SIGNS OF
MURDER

SIGNS OF MURDER

A Small Town in Scotland, a Miscarriage
of Justice and the Search for the Truth

DAVID WILSON

SPHERE

First published in Great Britain in 2020 by Sphere

1 3 5 7 9 10 8 6 4 2

A CIP catalogue record for this book
is available from the British Library.

Hardback ISBN 978-0-7515-7874-4
Export ISBN 978-0-7515-7873-7

Typeset in Warnock by M Rules
Printed and bound in Great Britain by
Clays Ltd, Elcograf S.p.A.

Papers used by Sphere are from well-managed forests
and other responsible sources.

Sphere
An imprint of
Little, Brown Book Group
Carmelite House
50 Victoria Embankment
London EC4Y 0DZ

An Hachette UK Company
www.hachette.co.uk

www.littlebrown.co.uk

For my sisters Alison, Annie and Margaret,
and in memory of Margaret McLaughlin

Prologue

Thursday 5 July 1973 had been like most other days in Carluke, a small Scottish town of around ten thousand people located between Lanark and Wishaw, connected to Glasgow by rail. Thursday had been just like Wednesday 4 July, which had been no different from Tuesday 3 July, and as people in the town were getting ready to go to bed they knew that pretty soon it would be Friday 6 July which, in turn, would be much the same as the day before.

One day seeped into the next.

Nothing much ever happened in Carluke, although at least the Highland games planned for that Saturday promised to disrupt the safe, monotonous civic rhythm that had come to pattern the lives of the townsfolk.

Even so, it had been a strange summer.

A total solar eclipse had occurred on 30 June and had lasted for over seven minutes. The newsreader said that the last time that had happened had been in 1098, and then, with a smile, explained that the next time an eclipse would last as long would be in 2150. President Nixon, who'd been inaugurated for his second term in January, was now caught up in something called 'the Watergate scandal' and was being threatened with impeachment, and the Provisional Irish Republican Army had begun a bombing campaign in London. David Bowie had only two days earlier retired his alter ego Ziggy Stardust at London's Hammersmith Odeon, and that spring all five nations who made up the rugby championship had each finished with four points. That had never happened before.

In truth, all of this seemed to pass Carluke by, and life there continued pretty much as it always had – much in the same way that summer always followed spring and night followed day.

So, in Glenburn Terrace Margaret McLaughlin was preparing for the last day of the working week, all the time dreaming about her impending marriage as she carefully laid out the clothes she would wear to Motherwell Post Office the following morning. She was planning to take the train into Glasgow after work to visit her future sister-in-law.

Her near neighbour George Beattie had just started his night shift at Lanarkshire Steelworks in Craigneuk and, being the obliging sort, he'd later agree to pick up tomatoes for his work colleagues to eat on their Friday night shift during one of their breaks.

William Muncie – one of Carluke's most famous sons – was secretly plotting how to capitalise on his reputation as 'Scotland's top detective', and so rise even further up the ranks of the police, before he had to retire.

Like Margaret, Maureen Weston, who'd been at school with George, was thinking about her wedding. That Thursday night she joked to her friend Elizabeth that she'd never seen the town so busy, with all the people coming and going in preparation for the Highland games. It was, she said, what people wanted to discuss when they came into Carluke's post office, where Maureen worked.

In Unitas Crescent, which bordered Glenburn Terrace, Laura Allan had all but given up her dreams of being an air stewardess and was starting to imagine what her life at Motherwell Technical College was going to be like. She had applied to start there at the end of the holidays, but meanwhile she would go to bed early so as to get a good night's sleep, before going back to her summer job at Stevenson's, a small general grocer's shop in the town. Although she didn't know it then, one day Laura would own a café in Carluke, which would come to serve as an informal community centre.

Margo Smith was reflecting on a good day's training in and around Colonel's Glen, and thinking about getting an early night too, for she had entered the hundred metres at the Highland games. The race was less than forty-eight hours away and she was determined to beat her main rival.

On the other side of town, Alison, Annie and Margaret Wilson were also getting ready for bed. Alison and Margaret still lived with their parents and their brother, but Annie had recently married and moved to another house in Carluke. Alison had just returned home, having given up her training as a nurse, explaining to her parents that she couldn't stand the hierarchy that dominated hospitals. She told her younger sisters that too, but her advice fell on deaf ears – both Annie and Margaret would become nurses and have long and successful careers.

And upstairs in his bedroom, their teenage brother was

3

drifting off to sleep, surrounded by books, with passages that he thought were especially important carefully underlined in pencil, and totally unaware that nearly fifty years later he'd be studying the events of the next few days in the hope of discovering the truth about a murder.

On Friday night, Carluke's safe, close-knit community was to be ripped apart by a shocking act of violence – the effects of which still ripple through time and space.

That strange summer was about to become still stranger, and much, much closer to home.

The Road Ahead

This is a story of home and of elsewhere; of the familiar and of those things which are alien; of coming, going, remembering and inevitably of returning home again.

It is about the past, the present and, hopefully, about the future too.

It is also a story about my home, and about Scotland.

I have used the word 'story' twice in these first few lines, but this is not a novel. What I am going to describe is all too depressingly real. At its heart this is a book about a murder – a single act of deadly malice that robbed a young woman of her life; a brutal and bloody murder that happened so quickly and in such a frenzy that no witnesses saw it happen, or caught sight of the blood-spattered culprit scuttling away.

Murder in all its bizarre, mass, multiple, serial and other guises has been such a feature of my life as a criminologist that it may seem strange to focus on this one case, but a sense of duty continues to sustain my interest in what happened in this particular murder. Duty implies some legal or formal obligation, but in that sense I have none. The duty that I feel is more informal and personal, and it is these particular interests, as much as my professional background, which drove my desire to return to my home town of Carluke. I returned because I wanted to try to make sense of what happened in the past, in the place where I once lived, and about the people who, at that time, shaped my existence. I didn't realise it at the time, but the personal archaeology at the heart of my journey was going to raise some uncomfortable questions.

My work with violent offenders – many of whom committed murder – means that there are professional accountabilities at stake here too. My career has been concerned with understanding violence and when, by whom, in what ways, and against which victims it will be used. Sadly, I have come to know all about the harm that some men can inflict on women.

So the personal and the professional combined and became for me the momentum to try to solve the mystery of a murder that has endured since I was a boy.

Not that the various statutory bodies that make up the Scottish criminal justice system see things in this way. For them there is no mystery. A man was arrested and charged with this murder – and eventually found guilty by a jury of his peers. All of his appeals against the conviction, the most recent in 2009, have been unsuccessful. As far as anyone 'official' is concerned, the murder that I am going to describe has been 'solved'; end of story, roll the credits and play the music.

Indeed, given that I am writing about events that took place nearly fifty years ago, the 'murderer' has now been released from prison and is now quietly living in Glasgow. His punishment, or so it is said, has ended.

That may be the official story, but don't be fooled. Theirs is a stubborn, 'trick ear' story, with a tunnel-vision detective playing the part of the unreliable narrator. That detective may have created a compelling and persuasive narrative that convinced a jury, but everything that he said was a fiction. I am going to show you that he was not dealing in facts; his persuasive narrative was not the truth. Even so, the criminal justice system continues resolutely, if passively, to deny that anything untoward has happened in the judicial process by refusing to acknowledge all the evidence to the contrary.

So then we must return to the personal, as opposed to the official, narrative and to my acute awareness that something happened in Carluke in 1973 that was deeply wrong and troubling, and which followed in the wake of an appalling and tragic murder, which was equally wrong and troubling. For I was sure then – as others were too – that the man they put in prison was wrongly convicted. 'Wrongly convicted'. That description is frankly far too polite; it's too mealy-mouthed, almost gracious. The blunt reality is that a man was 'fitted up'. This knowledge makes me as profoundly uneasy and uncomfortable now as it did at the time. How could we, as individuals and as a community, deny what we knew to be truth and collude in a fiction that was convenient, but ultimately incorrect? To have done so was to deny true justice.

Others share my unease, for I am constantly being asked to do something about this injustice when I return home, to make right what people describe to me as 'the Carluke case'. I've lost count of the number of times that someone has stopped me in the High Street, or approached me after I've given a talk at the library. Pleasantries will be exchanged and we will ask after each other's family; some kind comments will then be made about one of my books, or perhaps a recent appearance in the media. So far, so good. We both smile and at that point I think that I should be moving on. However, there will then come an almost imperceptible, hesitant pause indicating that something more needs to be said. I know what's coming next. The person will invariably look over their shoulder to check that no one is listening, then lower their voice and whisper: 'And can you not do something about the Carluke case?'

It's a heavy personal responsibility, but I must not be the only person to tell this tale. I need to make these other people in the town heard too – and not just in whispers, or behind closed doors for, as far as I am concerned, a rounded life cannot be lived in private. So I want to give a voice to the townsfolk who have willed me to write this book.

There is another aspect to the story, which has informed how I went about my research. I am aware of the name of the man whom many people in the town believe made a much likelier suspect than the one the criminal justice system convicted. In fact, his identity is an open secret and regularly discussed. That knowledge raises more responsibilities, both legal and ethical, which as a criminologist I take very seriously. However, I did not set out to 'prove' that this man is the murderer; that has not been my starting point in researching this case. I am not a vigilante, engaged in a witch hunt, or interested in listening to idle gossip. In any event, given that mine is not an official cold case review it would be impossible for me to prove guilt. I cannot gain access to the records of the original investigation, nor am I able to assess any forensic evidence that may still exist and have it subjected to new forensic tests. I cannot look at which suspects the police had their eyes on, scrutinise their formal interviews and gain an insight into why they were subsequently ruled out of the investigation. I cannot test what their alibis might have been, and whether they really did prove that they were somewhere else when the murder took place. I would expect to be able to do all of this – and more – if the journey I was setting out on was being undertaken on behalf of the police, and so I can only travel so far. However, this does not prevent others with more powers than me travelling in my footsteps at a later date, and that possibility means that I have to be careful about how and what I reveal.

There is one way that I have approached this murder as I would when re-examining any cold case: I let my research take me in whichever direction it led. So, no matter what people in the town might have discussed about there being a more likely suspect I did not let that shape my thinking. In fact, at the start of my journey I was only aware of this man's name and knew almost nothing further about him – not even what he might have looked like; if he still lived in the United Kingdom; or, perhaps most important of all, whether he was alive or dead. This more likely suspect, as others saw him, was not my starting point.

There was also always a possibility that my research would lead me back to the man convicted of the murder, but from even the little I knew at the outset, I felt that this was unlikely. However, and to be clear, if in the course of my research I uncovered evidence that might definitively prove that the courts had convicted the right man, that would have given me, and I think the community of Carluke too, just as much closure on the case.

9

My starting point was to fully understand the murder and then this man's conviction.

I also have to be sensitive.

I made a conscious choice not to interview either the victim's family or the man who was wrongly convicted of her murder. What would be the point of raking over these tragic embers? What new insights would such interviews deliver? All the materials that I therefore use and especially relating to the subsequent miscarriage of justice are already in the public domain. In fact, this ready visibility is what makes 'the Carluke case', and the lack of interest from official bodies, much more tragic.

After this starting point, my subsequent research was dominated by asking the next and most obvious question that flows from such a case: if the man who was convicted didn't kill this victim, then who did commit the murder?

What you are going to read is my investigation to try to answer that question and therefore discover the truth; the artless and ugly truth of who it was that took a young woman's life in Carluke in 1973. That search is in all of our interests – not just in Carluke, or in Scotland, but much more broadly. After all, no criminal justice system can exist in a 'post-truth' world, for matters of guilt or innocence really are about facts, which shape and then define what is right, and what is wrong. So these thorny, complex, personal and professional responsibilities which I have described, and which create a relentless tension in what follows, need to be managed, rather than shirked and evaded.

Truth, after all, is rarely easy and so makes demands of us all.

This awful murder in a small Scottish town and from a long time ago remains one of the most important in British history. That's a claim that I believe can stand any scrutiny, despite all the other miscarriages of justice which have happened within the criminal justice systems of the United Kingdom. This case is not just about the personal tragedy that murder always leaves in its deadly wake, but the wider tragedies that come when individuals and communities are disempowered and so learn to live within a culture of silence, or denial; when police incompetence and corruption is not just commonplace, but accepted as the norm; when investigations are premised on confirmation bias and convenience, rather than discovering the truth; when lies, conspiracy and official intransigence come to dominate the judicial process; and when power is concentrated in just a few hands and is exercised inappropriately in defence of a shabby, flawed, convenient but malfunctioning status quo.

The road ahead is long.

My research took place over two years, and what follows narrates each twist and turn, ventures down every blind alley, walks through the murder site, discusses the violence that was used there and who might have used it, and finally climbs the hills to get a better view of the entirety of the landscape. We might even stop off for a drink some time along the way. The road won't be easy; it is often daunting, depressing – in places demoralising, as murder is apt to be. But remember the old adage that travel broadens the mind, and so I urge you to join me, for the journey is going to be worthwhile and necessary – it's really the only way to heal the wounds of the past.

Oh, and just in case it has slipped your notice, it also means that a killer has still to be brought to justice.

CHAPTER ONE

The Murder

'A quiet girl'

It was Friday 6 July 1973 and the end of another working week. Like most twenty-three-year-olds, Margaret McLaughlin was looking forward to the start of the weekend and spending some time in Glasgow, away from her home in Carluke. She wasn't going to attend the Highland games. There was a lot for her to do and to think about; Margaret's life was changing and the world was beginning to open up before her. Her fiancé, Bob Alexander, was a young, successful businessman who happened to be working that summer in South Africa. Bob lived in Bearsden, in the north of Glasgow, which was one of the wealthiest areas not just in Glasgow, or Scotland, but in the whole of the UK. He had bought Margaret a rather splendid engagement ring which, unsurprisingly, had been shown off with some pride around Margaret's home town.

During the week Margaret was employed as a typist at Motherwell Post Office, where her elder sister Jane also worked. Apart from Jane, she had three other siblings, including two brothers – John and Edward. John, the eldest, had already moved away from Carluke and was working in a branch of Lloyd's Bank in Watford. The last of her siblings was her younger sister Rosemary, who worked in a shop in Glasgow.

Rosemary was going out that evening too and normally the two sisters would have travelled together. However, Rosemary had to catch an earlier train and so had left Margaret at home talking to their parents, Hugh and Jean. Their father had been unwell and was recuperating, but Jean had still helped Rosemary and then Margaret get ready for their respective nights out, and had even given Margaret some spending money for the weekend.

Margaret was travelling into the city to stay with Muriel, Bob's sister, soon to become her sister-in-law. Margaret must have been excited, as they were going to make some plans for the wedding; she also wanted to return a pair of trousers that she had bought in the city that didn't quite fit. Before leaving the house she had placed the trousers in a carrier bag and then put that bag into a small tartan suitcase, which she would carry with her to the station and then on to Glasgow.

Margaret said goodbye to her parents and left their house at 30 Glenburn Terrace at 7.52 p.m. to catch the 8.03 train from Carluke to Glasgow. It would still have been light at that time of the evening in July and so Margaret would not have needed a torch to guide her. The walk from her home to the station would only have taken her a few minutes as there was a well-used shortcut through an area of wooded ground, known locally as 'Colonel's Glen'. Glenburn Terrace was connected to another street, Unitas Crescent, and both were part of the same pool of council-owned properties that had been built to house the growing number of working-class families in the town, most of whom had come to work in the mines, or in the steelworks.

It was a close-knit area; the sort of place where kids played out in the street and everyone knew everyone else's business.

Two of Margaret's neighbours were sixteen-year-old Laura Allan, who lived at 36 Unitas Crescent, and Margo Smith, who lived at number 27. Laura had just left Carluke High School – known by everyone locally as 'the big school' – and had applied to go to Motherwell Technical College after the summer to do a secretarial course, having shelved dreams of becoming an air hostess. Margo was a year younger than Laura and a champion sprinter who would spend her days training in Colonel's Glen to get ready for the competitions she entered. On the Saturday, when Margaret was expecting to return her trousers to the shop in Glasgow, there was to be a Highland games in Carluke and Margo was going to run the hundred metres. Years later both of them fondly remembered that Glenburn Terrace and Unitas Crescent had been 'good places, where you could leave your front door unlocked. There was a real sense of community, where everyone knew one another.'

Even though she was a few years older and 'a very pretty, somewhat reserved Catholic girl', both Laura and Margo knew Margaret.

After leaving the house, Margaret turned right at the end

of Glenburn Terrace, heading north along Unitas Crescent which, as the name implies, forms an arc meeting the terrace at both eastern and western ends. As well as her suitcase, Margaret also carried a brown suede bag, slung over her shoulder, and a black umbrella, which she opened almost as soon as she had left the house, to protect her against the evening's shower.

The rain was heavy enough to swell the small and sluggish stream in the glen. That's an important point to bear in mind. The rain meant that the children who had been in the area had abandoned their play and instead sought shelter indoors, leaving the often noisy glen isolated and empty. Margaret's vision would also have been slightly obscured by her umbrella. According to one neighbour, who saw Margaret at the very start of her journey to the station, the wind was strong enough that evening to blow her umbrella inside out and she had had to pause to sort it out. The wind would also muffle sound.

An informal path cut between two semi-detached houses in Unitas Crescent led across an open area of ground before the entrance to the glen. The undergrowth that July was quite high and so grass and nettles bordered the path. Turning west and climbing a rather steep slope, was the railway embankment. If you followed the embankment you would quite quickly come to Carluke's station.

West Avenue lies just to the north of the station, and further north from there lies Stevenson Street and the Old Wishaw Road.

These were the streets that Margaret was preparing to leave behind, if only she had got to the station.

She never emerged from the glen to board the train.

The order and predictability of the everyday was broken that night and would come to provide an unlikely backdrop to an awful descent into savagery.

A black-and-white photograph of Margaret from around this time shows her smiling broadly at the camera and unselfconsciously fixing the viewer in her gaze. She looks confident, happy and optimistic about the future; she's a young woman on the verge of the rest of her life – the life that comes after school and childhood and living with your parents. Margaret wasn't just travelling into Glasgow that night, but also getting ready to move on from Carluke. Her life with Bob was going to be different to the one which she had been leading with her parents and her siblings in Glenburn Terrace.

Sadly, murder always holds about it the tantalising torment of what might have been.

The photograph in which she was smiling so optimistically was the one that her parents later gave to the police, in the hope of jogging the memories of witnesses. It was an expectant image in the wake of tragedy. One newspaper that reproduced the photograph captioned Margaret's image with 'a quiet girl'.

A phone call from Muriel later that evening alerted everyone to Margaret's non-arrival in Glasgow and an initial search by police officers, after Margaret had been reported as missing, took place at approximately 4 a.m. on Saturday 7 July. Her body was later found – the exact timing is still a matter of some dispute – towards the foot of Colonel's Glen, about thirty to fifty yards from the path up to the railway embankment and only about four hundred yards away from her home.

Margaret had been subjected to a ferocious attack.

Her umbrella was found damaged, lying some five or six yards to the right of the path, and, after the area had been cleared by the police on Sunday 8 July, Margaret's 'pinkie' ring was also discovered, although not her engagement ring. Her tartan suitcase, shoulder bag, wallet and toilet bag were recovered from the stream, some distance away from her body, where a pool had formed as a result of the rain. A knife was also found on the left of the path, beside a broken cement post. At the time, this was believed to have been the murder weapon. The knife was duly sent off for forensic testing.

There was blood spatter at various points on the path and in the glen, indicating the frenzied nature of the attack that had occurred.

As distressing as it is, we also need to consider more forensically how Margaret was killed, so as to gain some understanding of who her killer might have been, by describing how he went about this deadly business.

Margaret had been punched about the face and stabbed nineteen times. These stab wounds were distributed across her upper arms, chest, abdomen, back and the back of her neck. This pattern suggests that she had attempted to fight back, and then flee from her assailant. The wounds to her upper body penetrated the chest wall and thereafter her lungs, and the wounds to her abdomen pierced her liver, stomach and kidneys. As might be imagined from such a brutal attack, there was a great deal of internal haemorrhaging.

There was no evidence of sexual assault or post-mortem mutilation, nor was Margaret's body posed after her death. There was no real attempt to hide her body by burial or any other means, and no evidence that her killer had attempted to move her body from the glen to another site where it could be disposed of later. However, she did seem to have been dragged from the path, through the undergrowth and down the slope towards the stream.

Margaret was undoubtedly dead within a few minutes of the attack taking place.

Her killer would have been covered in her blood.

*

There was an initial and overwhelming sense of disbelief that a murder could have happened in the town. Everyone knew Colonel's Glen and there was hardly a man, woman or child who hadn't used the railway to travel to Lanark, Wishaw, Motherwell or Glasgow to go shopping, get to work, or go to school. Soon after the disbelief came fear. A murderer was at large – I remember that my father started to drive my sisters to and fro, rather than let them walk about the town. All that anyone seemed to do was talk about the murder, offer theories as to who had done it, worry that the murderer might be about to strike again, and wonder when the police were going to catch Margaret's killer.

The Saturday and Sunday after the murder saw the police begin to clear the area around the glen and start their house-to-house enquiries, building up a picture of who Margaret was and who might have wanted to see her dead. Gathering this type of intelligence takes time and drains the police of valuable resources – so much so that the Lanarkshire police drafted in help from the Scottish Crime Squad. These enquiries might be time-consuming, but they are a vital cog in bringing a culprit to justice, as it is usually the case that the victim and the perpetrator knew one another.

On Monday 9 July, three days after the murder, an aerial photograph of the general area was published in the *Daily Record*, Scotland's most popular daily newspaper. These photographs had been taken from a plane either chartered or owned by the paper and, as well as Bill Brown, the photographer, the plane also contained Detective Chief Superintendent William Muncie – 'Scotland's top detective'.

Muncie himself hailed from Carluke and he had quickly taken charge of the investigation. As for his flight, he was quoted at the time as saying that 'this has been invaluable ... I thank the *Daily Record* for their efforts in taking me on the aerial tour'. He further claimed that it had given him the 'chance to see the glen and the railway track in true perspective'.

Quite quickly Muncie developed some views about the attack and Margaret's killer.

On the front page of the newspaper Muncie suggested that Margaret's killer had subjected her to a 'frenzied attack'; that there was no indication of sexual assault and therefore 'the attack was motiveless' (reflecting thinking of that time); and finally, 'I feel sure some household must have noticed someone arriving home with signs of murder on his person. In kindness to that family, I appeal to them to come forward. It may well be that the killer needs attention and he could strike again.' These comments seem precise and crafted, almost to the extent that they had already been constructed on the basis of the local intelligence that had been gathered in the town. Who was this family that Muncie wanted to come forward? What sort of 'attention' was Muncie implying the killer needed?

Muncie was using the press to spread the local intelligence

more widely, and in doing so offering us a glimpse of his thinking about the case.

*

Muncie had been born in Carluke in 1915 and joined the police in 1936. Just under six feet tall, he had broad, muscular shoulders and a small moustache ornamented his top lip. This gave him a cheery, military look. Muncie has been described – as senior police officers often are and perhaps have to be – as 'wily and shrewd', but his police colleagues also described him as genial, with a ready smile and a passion for oil painting, horse racing, ornithology and wildlife. He was also, by all accounts, ruthlessly ambitious and loved publicity. Photographs from this time often show Muncie smiling benevolently but with confidence at the camera, almost as if he's daring the viewer to disagree. Wearing an overcoat, shirt and tie, with a hat on his head and a cigar in his hand, he strikes me in this pose as a rather more sophisticated, Scottish version of the fictional TV detective Columbo.

Perhaps Muncie is best summed up by one elderly local lawyer that I spoke to, who simply stated that 'I knew him by his reputation'. That's the sort of man that Muncie was and, to all intents and purpose, has remained – someone formed by his reputation.

His reputation was, above all else, shaped by murder.

Over the course of his career Muncie investigated and solved over fifty murder cases and 'the Carluke case' was to be his last. It was the final murder that he would investigate before his promotion to Assistant Chief Constable.

Muncie employed a particular and idiosyncratic method in going about his detective work. He would decide which suspect was guilty and then doggedly search for the proof to make his case. Later he came to say that he had almost 'psychic' powers for catching killers. Today we would call this type of approach 'confirmation bias'. However, his method worked in 1967, when Muncie brought Gordon Hay, the killer of Linda Peacock in Biggar, to justice, and again two years later when he secured the conviction of a lorry driver's mate called James Keenan for the murder of his wife Linda. Keenan had killed and then cut up his wife before scattering her body parts throughout south-east Scotland. At the end of his trial Ronald Murray, QC stated that Keenan's conviction had been the result of 'very thorough and painstaking police inquiries'.

In particular, while he was still a relatively junior detective Muncie had brought the criminal career of the American-Scottish serial killer Peter Manuel to an end. A rapist and murderer of at least seven people, the press named Manuel 'The Beast of Birkenshaw'.

Manuel's killings went on over a five-year period, and he was only caught because it was commented upon in the bars that he frequented that he seemed to have too much money to spend. The police managed to recover some of the money that he had spent and were able to trace the notes back to one of his victims. After his arrest, when taking detectives to show them where he had buried another of his victims, he casually remarked, 'This is the place. In fact, I think I'm standing on her now.'

Muncie seems to have relentlessly dogged Manuel through-out the latter's criminal career. He would later say that you needed to have patience to catch a killer. His patient, persistent pursuit of Manuel, and Muncie's belief that the

'Beast of Birkenshaw' was involved in every major incident that occurred, was described by his contemporary police colleagues as 'Manuelitis'. The fact that Muncie would eventually be proven correct gave him the confidence to use this approach more generally during other murder investigations. Manuel, of course, thought this was victimisation. So much so that he would eventually threaten Muncie and, in a letter that he tried to send to the detective but which was intercepted, he stated: 'He is going to get it. Next time you see him remind him that he has a wife and kids. He will understand.' He would also send birthday and Christmas cards to Muncie. Characteristic of the arrogance shown by many serial killers, Manuel refused legal representation and defended himself in court, but in any event he was found guilty. His last words before being hanged were reputedly 'Turn up the radio, and I'll go quietly.'

No matter what happened during Muncie's murder investigation in Carluke, it would be wrong not to acknowledge his long and successful career, and also the personal dangers that he had once faced.

*

Given this professional policing history and his maverick personality, the press loved Muncie and he in turn loved the press.

Senior detectives all have good reason to cultivate a working relationship with the media. It is the press, after all, that keeps the murder victim in the public's eye; it is the press that helps to nudge people's memories and so bring witnesses, or other forms of information, forward. Without a doubt, the media can be a valuable tool in bringing a perpetrator to justice. That said, there has to be a professional boundary between what the police and the press do, even if that professional boundary can, and often does, create tensions.

One such tension is the need to deliver results.

The media, quite naturally, want a story that grows; they like a whodunnit, with twists and turns that will keep their audience hooked. As the old newsroom saying goes, 'if it bleeds, it leads', and with the charisma of an investigator like Muncie there was no doubt that Margaret's murder, and the search for who had committed it, was going to be a story that ran and ran. After all, she was what criminologists would later come to term an 'ideal victim'. In other words, as a young, white, heterosexual female, she deserved our sympathy. She was someone whom the public could identify with and so they could see in her and the story of her life their own sister, mother, the girl next door, their former girlfriend. She was also reserved and quiet – cultural code for what was known about her sexual history, with the implication that she didn't 'sleep around' and therefore, as some would have seen it, she did not 'deserve' what had happened to her. In short, Margaret's victim status was legitimate, and this legitimacy made her murder all the more dramatic, sensational and newsworthy.

But there are dangers. Some murder detectives see involving the media in a case as like having a tiger by the tail. There's always a 'need to feed the beast' on a regular basis and sometimes there just isn't anything to give them that might sate their appetite. When that happens, some sections of the media will simply start to investigate the murder themselves, with the danger that this could seriously jeopardise the outcome of the case. When the media behaves in this way it also serves to undermine the general reputation of the police and, more often than not, specific detectives. Reputations that have been assiduously constructed by the media over time can just as easily be destroyed.

In the late 1950s and the early 1960s 'big, bad' John Du Rose, dubbed Scotland Yard's top murder detective, had been built up by the English press as the iconic 'four-day Johnnie' – the speed with which he was reportedly able to solve a murder case. It was an image that seemed to serve everyone well, and especially Du Rose. However, he would come unstuck after he had been asked to take charge of the investigation into a series of murders of sex workers in Hammersmith and Chiswick in the 1960s, attributed to a serial killer called 'Jack the Stripper'. With the nation watching on, 'four-day Johnnie' couldn't solve the case and 'Jack the Stripper' has never been caught. John Du Rose's reputation never recovered. He retired shortly afterwards, never gaining promotion to the most senior ranks of the police.

Muncie was aware of all of this, and there was yet another reason that he had to be careful. Even though he had reached the higher ranks of the police, he was ambitious for still further promotion. Margaret's murder would give him an ideal stage to show everyone just how talented he was. Her death became for him a canvas on which to display his supposed policing brilliance. I get the sense that he felt he deserved promotion; it was what he expected. After all, he had come to believe that he had almost supernatural powers in detecting who had committed a crime, and had brought the appalling Manuel to justice. He was Scotland's top detective; a man who knew how to get what he wanted; a man who got results.

This was the investigatory world in which this awful murder

in a small town would have to be solved, and the mindset of the detective leading the investigation. To our modern eyes, it doesn't look promising. There was no national DNA database or offender profiling to help; no CCTV cameras or Facebook pages to consult; and no mobile phone records to reveal who had last spoken with Margaret.

Yet it took only six days for the police to get their man.

So quickly did events unfold that the local newspaper, the *Carluke Gazette*, which was published every Friday, was never able to fully report on the case until much later.

So much for Muncie's love of patience, which he had claimed had brought Manuel to justice; Scotland's 'top detective' had struck gold again, but this time much more quickly.

Amongst all the police's back-slapping congratulations after the arrest, Margaret's family stoically laid her body to rest in Wilton cemetery on the other side of the town. Her gravestone simply stated that she lay 'in loving memory. Margaret Marie McLaughlin died 6th July 1973 aged 23 years, fiancée of Robert Alexander, daughter of Mr & Mrs Hugh McLaughlin.' Over time, first her father and then her mother would be buried in the same plot.

CHAPTER TWO

A Conviction

'with signs of murder on his person'

The girls counted out the numbers as they methodically cawed the skipping rope. Slowly at first, but then more quickly, their voices becoming increasingly shrill as the rope got faster and faster, until the jumper could no longer keep up and so tripped. It was good to get to twenty, but you had to be fit and have perfect timing to do that. The boys liked to think that they were the real athletes, kicking a football and dreaming of playing for Rangers or Celtic, but the girls could have shown them a thing or two – if only they'd been allowed.

Boys and girls didn't do that in Carluke in the 1960s; their sporting worlds were kept separate and Heaven help the boy or girl who crossed that unspoken boundary. To do so would mark you out as different and make you visible in a culture that might have been close-knit, but was also strictly divided by class, religion and gender.

Even so, some boys did.

George Beattie was a brakesman at Lanarkshire Steelworks in Craigneuk. He was nineteen and lived at 48 Unitas Crescent with his parents and three of his siblings. He also had four elder brothers who had all married and moved away from the family home. Given the proximity of Unitas Crescent to Glenburn Terrace it wasn't that unexpected that George would know Margaret, although there has never been any suggestion that they were particular friends, or that they were romantically involved. George doesn't seem to have been very interested in girls, even if he was known to have played with them as a child. Apart from the age difference between George and Margaret, there was also a religious divide. The Beatties were Protestant and the McLaughlins Catholic, and this simple fact meant that they had attended different schools.

Not that George had had much schooling. He had been kept back a couple of years at primary school and it was generally accepted that he had a below average IQ. A clerical error had then resulted in his leaving Carluke High School – 'the big school' – a year earlier than he should have; he didn't complain.

George was known about the town as someone who told 'tall tales', or, if you wanted to be unkind, he was a 'bullshitter'. He lived in a fantasy world. He liked to try to impress people, and was eager to please as a way of being accepted socially; he hated conflict. On leaving school he had held a variety of jobs, including as a hotel porter and working in a local laundry, then in a sweet factory; at one stage he was even working as a lift boy in a large Glasgow department store. This involved him travelling by rail into Glasgow and sometimes he had encountered Margaret on the same train, when she was travelling to work in Motherwell.

I remember him, standing on the railway platform as he noted down the numbers of the trains that were passing through Carluke. George loved trains and had a model railway back at his house in Unitas Crescent. With the money that he earned he would buy model engines and coaches, and much of his reputation in Carluke was focused on his fondness of model trains and the fact that he was a trainspotter.

As all of this might suggest, George had often been the victim of bullying, as he was seen as being 'soft' and immature; he was an easy target.

Maureen Weston was the same age as George, and worked in Carluke's own post office, rather than further afield. She didn't need to catch a bus or a train to work, or rely on lifts from friends. They'd been at Carluke Primary together which, unsurprisingly, was always called 'the wee school'. She remembered George being surrounded by a circle of other children who would take it in turns to punch and kick him. George didn't appear to object, and Maureen recalled that he seemed to rather like being the centre of attention. It was a childish game that was meant to shame him, but he appeared to enjoy it, although this wasn't masochism but much more his desperate need to be noticed and included.

Laura Allan remembered George as a child too. She had never, ever seen George get angry and, as children, while the girls might have had concerns about playing with other boys, they didn't have the same worries with George. Margo Smith, meanwhile, remembered George as the type of laddie who was 'just a big softie'. Scandalously for some, he would sometimes take his turn cawing the skipping rope for the girls as they jumped and tried to reach twenty.

Even as an adult, George was viewed as different. He shared a locker at the steelworks with a man called Colin McClair, who said that he had a reputation for making things up, and William Campbell, a fellow brakesman, suggested that George would often exaggerate about his drinking habits, but 'we knew that they are all lies'. In fact, he didn't smoke and hardly ever drank alcohol, which perhaps further served to mark him out as different to his contemporaries.

George had no criminal record and had in the past offered, on a confidential basis, information to the police about thefts that had taken place in the town. Even so, he was quickly arrested and then charged with Margaret's murder.

George was the centre of attention again, with the police taking their turn to metaphorically punch and kick him.

To be fair to Muncie, there were a few red flags about George. He knew Margaret and had an intimate knowledge of the shortcut to the railway station. Without doubt Margaret knew the man who killed her and the nature of the attack, and how he had subsequently disappeared suggested that he lived close by. These factors would, of course, have led to the police interviewing George. His shift at the steelworks began at 10 p.m. and there was evidence that placed him near the scene of the murder at around the time that Margaret was attacked. He was seen in Unitas Crescent, heading in the direction of the railway station, at about 7.40 p.m. – before Margaret had left the house – and spotted by another witness in West Avenue at 8 p.m., heading towards Stevenson Street, and eventually to Gorry's Nursery in Old Wishaw Road at around 8.30 p.m. where, ever obliging, he had gone to buy tomatoes for his work colleagues.

This errand should have provided George with an alibi. Even if the distances between Unitas Crescent and the Old Wishaw Road are not that great, and therefore George does appear to have been in the area for longer than was necessary (if the timings of these sightings are accurate), there are witnesses to him undertaking his errand. Their evidence is therefore of importance. None of these witnesses on his journey before reaching Gorry's saw George acting strangely, or out of the ordinary, and none commented that he had, for example, blood on his clothes, or that he looked unduly troubled, or emotionally high and disinhibited. Mr Gorry himself, who sold George his tomatoes, did not notice anything unusual at all. The journey may have been short, but it was long enough to have made it impossible for George to have committed the murder, gone home to change, dispose of his bloody clothes and then re-trace his steps to Gorry's, all the time acting as if he had nothing to hide.

Laura had one further memory of George: he was 'always eager to please. He never started a conversation, but if you said something he'd always agree with you. If you said, "Oh I hate her," he would then say "So do I."' In other words, he wanted to agree with you, even if that meant he would embellish the truth.

True to form, George talked himself into becoming a prime suspect and that was all it took for Muncie, Scotland's 'top detective', to pounce.

*

George's interviews were conducted without a lawyer being present (although this was standard at that time) and must also be seen against the broader context of his vulnerable personality. This vulnerability would be magnified when his later interviews were conducted in Carluke's police station, rather than in his home. When being interviewed at the station he would be outside his comfort zone, where he would have felt supported and at ease, and so he would have been scared and anxious; his desire to please and avoid conflict – especially with people in authority – would have left him further exposed and defenceless. He had no one to turn to for advice or help. Further muddying the water, there are no recordings of these interviews and we can therefore only reconstruct them from what was later said by the key participants, and through what was noted down by the police at the time in their notebooks – or at least in those notebooks which have survived.

It is important here to have an understanding of the specific context in which each of these interviews took place, as well as understanding a little more about George's personality.

George's first interview was with DS Adam and DC Waddell, taken during their house-to-house enquiries on Saturday 7 July. It is a simple account of his movements on the night in question. As George explains:

At about 7.55 p.m. on Friday 6 July 1973 I left my home to go to Gorry's tomato houses to collect tomatoes. I do this weekly for my workmates. I went down the service road which leads from Unitas Crescent and up the railway bank. As I reached the top of the bank the 8.03 train passed going to Glasgow. I looked towards the station and I only saw one figure standing on the northbound platform. I think it was a man. I carried on down through the old stables and made my way to Gorry's. Here I collected nine single pounds of tomatoes. I left Gorry's and went up to Carluke where I got the bus to Lanarkshire Steelworks where I work. At no time during my walk from my house to Gorry's tomato houses did I hear anything or see anything suspicious.

DS Adam noted down that George had been wearing a blue blazer-style jacket on the night of the murder, and this jacket was subsequently taken by the police and subjected to forensic testing. Nothing incriminating was found.

So far, so good, although George – a teller of tall tales – couldn't resist suggesting to James Kelly, a neighbour, on the following day that 'I must have been one of the last to see her,' and then clarifying: 'I seen her on the path, but I never seen her at the station.' He had never mentioned seeing Margaret at all when he had been interviewed by DS Adam and DC Waddell. But Margaret's murder was, understandably, all that anyone was talking about in the town. George couldn't help himself and slowly but surely inserted himself into the story. He told a work colleague called Robert McAllister that he had seen blood at the scene of the crime in the glen, although he quickly explained that this was where boys skinned rabbits. When Robert had joked with him about where he had hidden the knife, George had replied that he didn't own a knife.

However, a knife had *indeed* been found near the crime scene. It was six inches long and just over an inch at its widest part; it had a wooden handle, which was hooked at the end.

It was later described as looking like the kind of knife that a butcher might use. It was found by PC John Baker along a path that led through the glen towards the station, and beside a broken cement post. Beyond the post, blood could be seen on the ground. PC Baker was told to leave the knife where it was and, under the direction of Muncie, the knife was photographed and then removed. In addition to removing the knife, soil from around it was also taken for examination. This was all done with some care and Muncie took the knife out of the soil in the presence of Walter Weir, a consultant pathologist, and William McLay, the chief medical officer, who both subsequently carried out the post-mortem on Margaret.

They offered an opinion to Muncie when they were still in the glen, that the wounds which Margaret had received could have been caused by the knife that was found.

This was quite clearly good news for the investigation; after all, Margaret had been repeatedly stabbed. With that in mind, the knife was sent off for forensic testing on Monday 9 July.

As can be inferred, the finding of the knife and its subsequent handling were treated with great care, given that this was believed to have been the murder weapon. This is as it should be, and sending the knife for further testing was standard practice at this time, as it would be now. Of course there was no DNA analysis available, but the forensic testing would have been able to show if any blood on the knife, or in the soil, had belonged to Margaret and/or her killer, which would have allowed the police to narrow down their pool of suspects.

Muncie must have believed that Margaret's killer had deliberately left the knife where it was found, after he had completed the murder. He had driven it into the soil beside the cement post, perhaps as a way of cleaning blood from the weapon. This was another form of evidence that could be used to narrow down the pool of suspects – Margaret's killer would have known where he left the knife, what it looked like and what he had done with it after the murder had been completed. It is obvious that a great deal of evidentiary value was being ascribed to the finding of the knife and what a suspect might say about a knife.

Carluke is a small town. The sort of small town where George's conversations with neighbours, friends and work colleagues would have quickly got back to the police investigating the appalling murder of a young woman. The sort of place where, as the contemporary website, the Knowhere Guide, puts it, 'if someone fell and hurt their knee at the bottom of the town, by the time they got to the top of the town everyone would be saying that the person has had their leg amputated'.

Thus what George said would have started to raise concerns, and these concerns would in turn lead to questions. Two plus two might just add up to more than four. After all, George had spoken about seeing Margaret and blood, and a work colleague had also joked with him about where he had hidden the knife. So perhaps, just perhaps, he had murdered Margaret too?

George was interviewed for a second time on Tuesday 10 July, again in his home by DS Adam and DC Waddell – an interview which was recorded in the latter's notebook.

This second interview provides a few further details. George explains that he had been wearing 'a fawn-coloured polo-necked sweater, blue jeans, black shoes and a navy blue suit jacket', and that he was carrying a red and blue bag to put the tomatoes in after he had collected them from Gorry's. He mentions other people whom he had seen on the night, such as Walter Mathers and Ian Friel, and Elizabeth Sirrell, who had been in her father's car. He also says that he slipped on the path in the glen and that he dropped the bag. He had had 'to put my foot on it to stop it sliding' back down the slope. He says that a small boy in the front compartment of the 8.03 train had waved to him, and that he had seen a man wearing a brown overcoat waiting on the station platform, although he did not recognise him.

But still George made no mention to the police of having seen Margaret, or indeed of noticing any blood.

*

George didn't seem to appreciate that he was quickly becoming the prime suspect in the investigation, and so, on that Tuesday evening, after giving his second statement, he agreed to reconstruct the journey that he had made to Gorry's. George walked with a limp, as he claimed that he had been hobbling on the night of the murder as he was carrying an injury. Did he do this to generate some sympathy from the detectives, or to imply that he was an unlikely killer? In turn, might the detectives have seen his injury as suspicious? In any event, DS Adam and DC Waddell followed on behind him as he limped from his home through the shortcut and into the glen, and then up the railway embankment. It must have been a pathetic sight. The weather was poor that night, and so the reconstruction was abandoned quite quickly.

We don't have much empirical evidence about this first, informal reconstruction but, during George's various appeals, the Crown were at pains to point out that all the various 'label productions' (Margaret's possessions) and Margaret's body had been removed prior to the reconstruction taking place. The Crown was trying to maintain that George's 'special knowledge' of the crime didn't come from being walked through the crime scene. However, we do not know what might have been said by either DS Adam or DC Waddell to George during this time, although it must have been sufficiently troubling as they asked him to come to Carluke Police Station the following day to make a further statement.

Limping or not, George was all the time edging himself further and further towards his fate.

There is some evidence to suggest that George might have been beginning to worry that the police's interest in his movements on the night of the murder was becoming a problem. He phoned James Gorry to order some more tomatoes and suggested that he was going to take the tomatoes to England, 'away out of the road', which Mr Gorry took to mean away from Carluke and the investigation.

Whatever this might have meant, and it could simply have reflected how frustrated he was becoming with the police's attention, George attended Carluke Police Station the next day.

Earlier that day – Wednesday 11 July – Muncie received a letter reporting on the forensic examination that he had requested about the blood found on the articles submitted by him for testing two days earlier. That letter made it clear that 'no human blood' had been found on the knife, or in the soil that the blade had been driven into. There were no traces of Margaret's, or indeed George's blood. In other words, this knife was unlikely to have been the murder weapon. This information does not seem to have been made available to any

37

of the officers interviewing George, and so the investigation proceeded in the belief that the knife was the murder weapon, and therefore knowledge of the knife and where it had been found could only have been possessed by Margaret's killer. In police jargon, this was the 'special knowledge' the Crown were at pains to demonstrate at trial.

At the station George again went over the statements that he had made, but this time he was interviewed by DC John Semple and PC Dennis Mair, rather than DS Adam and DC Waddell. It is unclear if DC Semple and PC Mair were aware that George had visited the murder scene in the company of the latter two detectives the previous evening. DC Semple and PC Mair would also have been conducting their interview in the belief that the murder weapon was the knife that had been found at the scene and so, as far as they were concerned, knowledge of the knife would be special knowledge that only Margaret's killer could know.

DC Semple started to sketch a map of the journey that George had made through the glen, marking points of interest as they cropped up during the interview. This was the first time that George was interviewed in the police station, as opposed to in his home – he was alone, with no solicitor, nor even a family member present, and therefore under much greater stress and even more eager to please because of it.

George provides much more information in this third interview. He says that he stopped for a pee and went behind a tree, but was unable to urinate. He said to the officers, 'I always pee here after I have left the house to go past the station or come to the wood ... I tried to pee that night but I couldn't. I must have been already.' He offered information that he would go into the woods to 'skin rabbits for the pot. I cut them up the middle with a linoleum knife that is a wee knife with just a small blade. I then cut off their feet with an axe. I cook the rabbits and then eat them.' This area was undoubtedly a place where local boys did catch and skin rabbits. He suggests that he heard a noise which frightened him and, as a consequence, he ran and tripped, which meant that he hurt his knee and cut his hand. He said that he noticed blood on the ground, but that could have been as a result of the rabbits being skinned. He states that he dried his hand on a paper hankie and put this in his pocket.

It is in this interview that George divulges a key new piece of information. He claims that he had heard something which had made him frightened – in his first statement he had made it plain that at no time did he hear or see anything suspicious. Did George actually become frightened on his walk to Gorry's, or was this simply said as a way of easing the pressure that he felt during the interview? His statements about rabbits being skinned and the knife that he would use to do so certainly seem to have been prompted by questions posed by DC Semple and PC Mair. Why mention a knife at all? Note too that George emphasises the shortness of the knife that he would use to skin a rabbit, which is markedly different from the knife which had been found near the crime scene. Even so, this must have raised the suspicions of the interviewing detectives that he had special knowledge – knowledge that only someone involved in the murder would possess.

DC Semple marked various points that were discussed on his sketch, but he and PC Mair were going off duty. The responsibility to continue to interview George fell to DS

Douglas Mortimer and DC Lewis Johnston, and DS Mortimer would continue to add to the sketch begun by DC Semple.

As he was going off duty, DC Semple told DS Mortimer that George didn't really understand what he was saying and seemed to be adding to his statement for the sake of talking, concluding that he was a 'bit simple' and 'not really normal'. DC Semple was making it plain that it was difficult to trust what George was saying. Indeed it is obvious that the statements that George made about going for a pee behind a tree, and how he always did this when he left his house to go to the station, were childish nonsense. In fact he immediately contradicted himself by saying that he couldn't urinate, as 'I must have been already.'

It was a long night and George would be interviewed by a series of detectives as one shift ended and another began. George didn't get to go 'off duty' like his interviewers but instead continued into a new interview – this time with DS Mortimer and DC Johnston. He was still alone and perhaps still unaware of the perilous situation that he was in.

It is at this point that George tied himself inextricably to the crime – at least in the eyes of his interviewer.

Recorded in those police notebooks, which were later described in court, it is reported that George begins to describe not only where Margaret's body had been found but also items of her clothing that she had packed into her suitcase, and he even states that he had tripped over the umbrella that she had been carrying. In what seems like a response to George's descriptions, DS Mortimer went each time to the productions room in the police station and brought back the exact piece of clothing that George had mentioned and which

40

had been collected at the murder scene. George described having seen 'something blue and white which could have been trousers'; a 'white goonie' [nightgown]; and 'a small tin or jar or bottle of hair spray'. DS Mortimer found all of these items in the productions room and, as they had been in Margaret's case, George could only have seen them if he had seen the case open.

George had managed to place himself at the scene of the crime, and to provide information that seemingly only the killer would know. Even at this point it's unlikely he knew where all of this was leading, and what he said must be seen within the context of his being tired and increasingly distraught, but still eager to please and avoid conflict.

Indeed, at the culmination of their interview DS Mortimer states that he had asked George if he was certain that he hadn't seen Margaret on the night that she had been murdered, at which point George began shaking and sobbing. He then admitted: 'I saw her. She had her umbrella in her left hand and her suitcase in her right hand', and that he had run after her to help her to carry her case. At this point George was cautioned.

It was late at night and several hours since the interviews had first started. George's emotional stress would not have been eased by being formally cautioned. He was tired – they were all tired. But then George became hysterical, and made an even more extraordinary statement:

They telt me they were going to cut me up into sardines if I telt the police. There were six of them. Three came down from the banking, three from the wood side. Two of them were wearing tall hats with mirrors or glass in them. The tallest man held her. I felt sick. They poked me with umbrellas and made me watch.

George spoke about the men stabbing Margaret time after time and being made to watch what was happening to her. George spoke so quickly that DS Mortimer was unable to note everything down; he started to sob again and then put his arms around DC Johnston. He was obviously emotional and was described as having a minor epileptic fit.

At 1.30 a.m. George was charged with murder.

After being charged George replied, 'I canny say no more. I didn't do it. It was they six.'

Later, George would say that the story about men wearing tall hats with mirrors on them, poking him with an umbrella and forcing him to watch Margaret being murdered, had actually been suggested to him, but by then it was too late.

At no point in all of his time in custody did George ever admit to the murder. Despite all the pressures that he came under, he steadfastly maintained his innocence. His original lawyer, who, after George had been convicted, would visit him in prison, said that 'George always maintained his Not Guilty plea. He never once said to me that he was guilty.'

No one believed that the six men George talked about in this 'pseudo-confession' had killed Margaret – it soon became clear that the reference to the two wearing tall hats with mirrors was probably an allusion to the pop group Slade. It all seemed too fantastic; it all seemed, well, just like George.

But while some people in the town might have been sceptical that George was the culprit, in Carluke more generally people seemed to accept this narrative and quietly got on with their business.

Only a few brave souls, and especially the Beattie family, chose to challenge the police's version of events.

CHAPTER THREE

The Flaws in a Flawed Investigation and the Need for Another

'the lone heron and the cunning old fox'

The facts of the case are clear: a young woman called Margaret McLaughlin was murdered; six days later a man was charged with committing that murder; a man who would eventually be found guilty of this crime by a jury of his peers and sent to prison.

It's a simple, almost reassuring narrative.

However, this narrative quite quickly breaks down under further investigation. A cursory glance at the statements made by George during his interviews raises a number of red flags and some serious questions. This isn't just said with hindsight; some were dissatisfied even at the time. The mood in Carluke might have been tense – the town had been torn apart and was reeling from the shock of losing a young woman in the most appalling of circumstances – but an understandable empathy for Margaret and her family, and a desire for a killer to be quickly behind bars did not deter a few people from distrusting the police's account. Even in 1973 some of the town's residents were prepared to question the speed with which a man had been charged with Margaret's murder, and others simply doubted that George Beattie – a well-known teller of tall tales, someone who avoided conflict and was always eager to please – could have been responsible.

The police would have been privately celebrating as there's nothing like getting a result and Scotland's top detective had struck again, but this is where we have to start questioning the conduct of the investigation and the quality of the information that saw George arrested, charged and convicted. We have to join the Beattie family and the few other brave souls who raised their heads about the town's civic parapet and question whether this was the right outcome, or simply a convenient one.

The place to start looking into all of this more critically is the man in charge of the investigation itself – Detective Chief Superintendent William Muncie.

We get glimpses of both the man and the detective in Muncie's memoirs, *The Crime Pond*, published in 1979, three years after his retirement. Though Muncie does not actually mention Carluke, or indeed the murder of Margaret McLaughlin (which is perhaps significant in itself), we do get some insight into Muncie as a police officer, and how his personality and professional career influenced his investigatory approach.

Muncie didn't think of himself as having had a crime 'patch' over the course of his career but rather, given his keen interests in fishing and birdwatching, a pond where various birds and animals would come to reside. He writes that:

> On the surface the pond presented a scene of quiet bliss, of calm and composure, of industry and ecstasy. But to an observer with a knowledge of the lives and habits of the pond's population it was a scene marred by the presence of troublesome marauders, thieves, pillagers and killers ... Is human life not like this? Lone killers are like the solitary heron – the patient killer of the marshes; the slightest move of a fish in the shallow end of the water and – like lightning – that heron would spring to life and makes its kill. Its success the reward of endless patience. Perhaps, in that respect, I had something in common with that heron?

But he wasn't content with just this analogy; later in the book, he compares himself to a 'cunning, old fox'.

Muncie did not see anything wrong with applying his keen observations of animal life directly to human behaviour and he admitted that, like some psychics, there had been strange incidents in his career, which he believed came from his special intuition. 'After all,' he says, 'mammals and birds have extra built-in senses.' Muncie came to accept that he had developed a unique understanding of crime and offenders, stating that 'even at the first of Peter Manuel's eight murders, I was convinced that he was the person responsible, and I was further convinced at each of his subsequent murders, though there was no evidence until the last of his crimes'. He had also been certain that Linda Keenan had been murdered by her husband James and, as he explains, he would eventually 'be proved right and was thereafter considered psychic'.

Muncie's observation is meant to suggest humility – it is other people who are saying this – but it is clear that he saw himself as a psychic too.

That's a worry, to put it mildly.

A belief that you have special intuition and can detect perpetrators that others would be blind to leads inexorably to confirmation bias. In other words, Muncie would interpret events so that they confirmed his existing beliefs, ignoring evidence to the contrary and which pointed in another direction. Even if on some occasions he was proven right, intuition alone is a precarious and dangerous basis on which to build an investigation, especially if there is in fact no genuine evidence to support your hypothesis.

In his memoirs Muncie also reflects on what it is that drives a man to murder, though he notes that 'we are no closer to an answer than we have ever had been (or are now)' and so calls for more research and study of the human mind. Yet he observes that:

some people with an aberration of mind have been found who quite openly declare a desire to kill, yet never even attempt to do so. But others, because they show no aberration, are to outward appearances normal; yet they are insane and are only found to be insane after they have murdered. By then it is just that little bit too late.

*

The unnamed author of the short introduction to the memoirs discusses Muncie's good relationship with the press in his time as Chief Superintendent, and how on his promotion to Assistant Chief Constable a group of reporters called him with their congratulations. But to ensure that the reader didn't get the impression that Muncie's relationship with the press had become too cosy, this anonymous author mentions that this same group of reporters said that they had been treated like 'mushrooms'; that they had 'been fed shit and kept in the dark'.

This hardly seems likely.

If this was the case, why would a group of them have wanted to acknowledge Muncie's promotion at all? Their congratulations are much more likely to be the culmination of a good relationship and their grateful thanks for all that he had done to help them in the past – and would hopefully continue to do for them in the future. The mushroom joke is simply another way of deflecting our attention from that relationship and serves to imply distance rather than intimacy. It's a verbal sleight of hand.

With this in mind we should again consider Muncie's willingness to fly in the *Daily Record*'s plane three days after the murder. It's likely he would argue that he was merely harnessing the power of the press to keep a murder investigation in the public eye. Even so, by using the media's resources rather than those belonging to the police, it does feel as if he had crossed a line.

More than any of this, we also have to question whether the publication of the photograph of the crime scene, indicating where Margaret's body had been found and where the police were still searching, impacted on the investigation by putting this information – 'special knowledge' – into the public domain. It is worth remembering that this photograph had been published on the Monday after the murder. George Beattie's first interview had been taken on the Saturday morning, during the police's first house-to-house enquiries and is a simple recounting of his movements. Greater detail is only offered by him in his subsequent interviews, when a great deal of information was by that stage swirling around Carluke, or had been put into the public domain by the police themselves.

Whatever the case – and there will be dissenting views about this – we also need to accept that through his desire to be at the centre of the unfolding investigation it was actually George himself who first offered himself up as Muncie's 'lone heron'. Thereafter it was Muncie's error in speedily accepting that this vulnerable young man had, like the heron, sprung to life to make its kill after spotting a fish in the shallow end of the pond. Once Muncie had him in his sights, he wasn't prepared to let George go.

It is here that we have to pause and consider the facts that I have outlined. It is obvious that there was something not quite right about how the police went about their investigation, and about the conclusion that they came to. My unease with their case against George bothered me – and others – at the time, and continues to cause considerable disquiet in the town today. There's something about 'the Carluke case' that just doesn't make sense.

Frankly, George is a very unlikely heron, as some people in the town immediately realised. I remember his arrest being discussed and a sceptical – if whispered – incredulity that it was remotely possible for him to be the culprit. Perhaps the most pertinent question to ask is why he was ever arrested and charged at all. The three major reasons that seem to have sealed his fate relate to the knife that was found and which was initially believed to have been the murder weapon; George's supposed special knowledge of the crime scene, which included where Margaret's body and possessions were found; and, finally, the extraordinary statements he made to the police – the last of which can be viewed as a 'pseudo-confession'.

Let's take a look at these reasons one by one, as a way of opening up Muncie's investigation and to begin the process of thinking about Margaret's murder afresh, as if it was a cold case.

*

First, we should consider the knife.

Knives, or to be more accurate a knife, were always going to be central to the police's investigation; after all, Margaret had been stabbed nineteen times. Identifying someone who might have routinely carried a knife – maybe because they used one in the course of their daily work – would have been a good starting point in their inquiry. I doubt that Margaret's killer had first encountered her and *then* decided to find a knife near the crime scene with which to attack her. It is much more likely that he was already carrying a knife when he came across her. I have used the pronoun 'he' as statistically we can assume that this type of attack was carried out by a man. Over 90 per cent of all murders are committed by men, and these men will usually be under thirty. The police could also have checked on local residents who had previous convictions for violence that involved using a knife and, without doubt, their door-to-door enquiries would have produced a great deal of local intelligence.

I couldn't find any evidence of specific information about those in the area who routinely carried knives. However, clearly there would have been some local intelligence, even if what was discussed with the police has disappeared from the historical record, or I simply couldn't access it because this was not an official cold case review.

The discovery of a knife just a few yards from Margaret's body was a key piece of evidence and a reasonable starting point in tracking down her killer. We know what that knife looked like, and where it was found. We know who discovered the knife, and how seriously its discovery was treated by Muncie, especially after he had been assured by the consultant pathologist and the chief medical officer that it could have been the murder weapon. We also know that the knife, and the soil that it was discovered in, was sent off for forensic testing on 9 July.

However, on 11 July the report on the knife came back to the Chief Superintendent.

It was devastating news for Muncie.

The report concluded that there was 'no human blood present' either on the knife or in the soil. The report suggested that 'for any future report for the procurator fiscal the above productions would have to be re-examined'. The idea that a further scientific investigation could form the basis of a 'future report for the procurator fiscal' might suggest that the investigation that had been undertaken had been preliminary and done to simply help Muncie progress his case. Again this is something which I am unable to determine, although it is obvious that the last thing that Muncie would have wanted would be another report of this kind. The absence of human blood was disastrous for his case. Even if George had 'cleaned' the knife, as might be inferred from some of his later interviews, for example, by driving it into the soil, he would not have been able to destroy all traces of human blood on the knife, or in the soil, without access to various chemicals. Even in the 1970s, the forensic tests that were used would have revealed the presence of human blood. No matter what offenders think and how careful they believe they are, they leave traces of themselves on their victims and on the weapons that they have used to kill their victims. Muncie clearly understood this too, which was why he had placed so much emphasis on the knife and the soil being sent off for testing.

In other words, the knife that had been found was not the murder weapon. But this crucial forensic report was never offered to George's defence, and it would take twenty years for it to come to light – in March 1993 – and even then only after a good deal of pressure from Carluke's MP.

So here's the unpalatable truth, and an insight into how confirmation bias works in practice. By 11 July 1973 Muncie knew that the knife that had been found close to Margaret's body was not the murder weapon. Muncie wasn't stupid. He knew that if no human blood had been found on either the knife or in the soil that it had been driven into, there was no evidentiary value in the knife – what it might have looked like, or where it might have been found. However, he didn't share this information – it didn't fit with his intuition and psychic powers and so the investigation proceeded as if the knife was still the murder weapon. As far as the police interviewing George were concerned, their working assumption would have remained that information about the knife and where it had been found could only have been known by Margaret's killer. These issues would become central to the interviews that George gave at the police station and in his final and extraordinary visit to the glen, where he would point out where the knife had been left.

Undoubtedly this supposed special knowledge played its part in his later conviction.

As I have explained, special knowledge is shorthand for knowledge that only the killer could have been aware of and privy to. It is therefore knowledge that the police will often keep out of the public domain so that they can quiz the surprising number of people who come forward to confess to crimes, especially murders. Sometimes this might be as simple as asking whether the victim was wearing shoes or if they were barefoot at the time they were killed. Depending on the circumstances of the murder, other seemingly banal questions can also be posed and can be used to rule out someone who is wasting the police's time. However, in the same way that someone can be ruled out of a murder inquiry by not having the requisite knowledge of the crime, someone who reveals accurate, crime-specific details when interviewed is clearly a person of interest and therefore a likely suspect.

It's easy to forget that the other group of people who have special knowledge of a crime are the police themselves.

Remember again that George emphasised the shortness of the knife that he would use to skin a rabbit. That was clearly said in the knowledge that the knife found at the crime scene, and which was still believed to have been the murder weapon, had been six inches long. How did George know that? Was it common knowledge, or perhaps shared by DS Adam and DC

Waddell on their journey through the glen? This is not meant to be unduly critical of the police. We now accept that interviews with vulnerable suspects have to be handled with care and that these interviews often involve the police – perhaps unconsciously – transmitting information to the suspect, as much as they might hope to receive information from the person being interviewed.

Even so, discussion about the knife here is irrelevant in proving guilt, as it was not the murder weapon. Instead, their exchange simply helps us to better understand where this special knowledge might have come from: the police themselves. George's comments about blood were more than likely an awareness that he had told people that he had seen blood at the crime scene, although, as in his conversation with Robert McAllister, he was at pains to point out that this was where rabbits were skinned. No doubt that was true; after all, there was no *human* blood on the knife. In looking at what George said more forensically and knowing something about his personality, it is hard to determine if he actually saw Margaret at all. In fact, in his first police interview on the Saturday he makes no mention of having seen her as he made his way to Gorry's. Perhaps this is as close to the truth as we can now get.

What is also true, and seems to have been disregarded by the police, is the fact that there were several witnesses who saw George as he carried out his errand for his work colleagues before starting his shift. Laura's father, William Allan, had even given him a lift home on the morning after the murder, at the end of their shift. George had not mentioned anything unusual to William, or revealed to him details that might have connected him to Margaret's death, although it

54

would now seem – as with the knife – that the defence were never made aware of these facts. No witnesses reported that George looked flushed, excited, or that he was acting out of the ordinary. He was not covered in blood, as Margaret's killer would undoubtedly have been, and, perhaps most crucial of all, no forensic evidence has ever been found to connect George to the murder – although there was some comment at the time by one or two police officers about a spot of blood that had been found on his handkerchief. There were no fibres from her clothes on what he was wearing; no scrapings of his skin under Margaret's fingernails. He didn't dispose of any of his clothes and nor were any of Margaret's stolen belongings ever found in his possession.

He had none of Muncie's 'signs of murder' on him.

So, the material evidence against George was very thin; so thin as to be non-existent. In fact, there was actually more evidence to support his *not* being involved in the murder, but that did not suit the narrative that Muncie had constructed.

Putting the knife aside, we still have to tackle the issues of George's statements and how, in his initial statement, he appeared to show special knowledge of the crime scene itself.

Looking at everything as a whole, it seems that his first two statements to the police are probably as close to the truth as it gets about what he *actually* knew. George's claim to have seen Margaret and blood on the path seems to have been invented later as a way of connecting him to everything that was happening in the town; it was a means to make him feel central and important. He was in the circle at the wee school again – a circle which had been designed to shame him, but where he quite liked the attention. Crucially, he'd said nothing to William Allan on the morning after the murder, and only started to speak about it after Margaret's death became a subject of local, and then national, interest.

George hadn't recognised that what he said, how he would change and augment his story to make himself important and significant, would also make him uniquely vulnerable.

Next we should consider George's first visit to the glen with DS Adam and DC Waddell, as this begins to open up the reason why he might have had special knowledge of the crime scene. Let's leave to one side that Muncie had flown with the *Daily Record* over the scene of an ongoing investigation into a murder, and that the newspaper had then published photographs of that scene on its front page. Let's also ignore that what had happened to Margaret – and where – was the talk of the town, and simply marvel at the fact that George was in effect being given a guided tour of the crime scene by two police officers, as much as he was recreating his own journey to Gorry's. At his appeal it was stressed that the various 'label productions' from the police production room and Margaret's body had been removed prior to this tour commencing but, even so, we do not know what the conversation between George and the two detectives might have been, or what other informal information might have been exchanged, perhaps by chance, during this trip to the glen.

Despite DC Semple's reservations about what George was actually saying, it was George's responses to questions posed by DC Mortimer that would lead to him being charged with murder. As might be imagined, this interview is the subject of great controversy. This controversy is not helped by the fact that DC Johnston's notebook, which could have verified – or contradicted – what was said to have happened, was destroyed by DC Johnston in the mid-1990s, after he had given an extensive interview about its contents to Peter Hill, the campaigning investigative reporter. It is hard to determine if Hill read the notebook, or took copies of it, or merely reported on what Johnston had said to him. This confusion is not helped by the fact that Johnston later stated that he had destroyed his notebook on the 'advice of his solicitor', although that solicitor has never been identified. Again, I have no access to any copies of this notebook, or what it might have contained beyond what Hill has described.

George's ability to incriminate himself didn't end with his statement to DS Mortimer in Carluke Police Station. At times, when reading about the case, it struck me that the Scottish police seemed to receive more confessions than the priesthood. As he was being driven on the night of his arrest from Carluke to the cells in Lanark, prior to his first appearance in court, George asked DS Mortimer if he wanted to know how the knife that was believed to have killed Margaret had been cleaned, after which he was again cautioned. He nonetheless offered to show the police where this had happened and so, in the morning, he was taken back to the glen for a second time, this time handcuffed to DC Johnston and in the company of DCS Muncie and DCI Gold, but still not in the company of a solicitor. Once more George found a way of incriminating himself with statements that he is alleged to have made to Muncie and other officers.

In essence, this package of special knowledge would become the Crown's case against George. He knew where Margaret's body had been left; where the knife that had supposedly killed her was to be found, what it looked like and how it had been cleaned; voluntarily described possessions that had been in her suitcase; and provided a pseudo-confession that to all intents and purposes admitted that he had been present when Margaret had been murdered. It was enough to convince a jury, albeit not by much.

According to Peter Hill, DC Johnston's destroyed notebook revealed a very different picture from the one that was presented at George's trial. Far from one item of Margaret's possessions after another being brought out of the production room in response to what George was saying, no such thing was recorded by DC Johnston. And, as viewers of the Netflix series *Making a Murderer* might recognise from how the Wisconsin police interviewed Brendan Dassey, George was seemingly being fed information, if Hill is correct, and that this was then repeated by him so that he appeared to be in possession of special knowledge. Study after study has shown that up to 90 per cent of false confessions by those accused of crimes, but who are later shown did not commit these crimes, contain accurate information.

Here we also need to remember that the knife that was believed to have killed Margaret was not in fact the murder weapon at all – although initially only Muncie seems to have been aware of this fact, and it looks like he kept this information to himself during the investigation. Later, at the trial, it is surely of more than passing interest that the prosecution did not call their forensic scientists as witnesses and that they were instead only called by the defence – to demonstrate that there was no forensic evidence to connect George to the crime scene. However, that does not seem to have impressed the majority of the jury, who seem instead to have been dazzled by George's pseudo-confession. So too that the route that Margaret had taken on the night she had been murdered, and even where her body had been found, had been published in the *Daily Record*. Many people in Carluke would have had similar 'special knowledge' to George, although he alone had also been given a guided tour of the crime scene, which undoubtedly added to his awareness of what had happened to Margaret. Nor did DC Johnston recall any incriminating conversations between George and Muncie – again the destroyed notebook would have clarified this point.

Most important of all, we should also remember that there was a complete absence of forensic evidence to link George to Margaret, despite Muncie's view that the killer would have 'signs of murder on his person'. There were no such signs on George, as a number of witnesses testified.

In my mind, the case against George is broken – there *is* no case. Indeed, the more I looked into these matters, the more convinced I became that George had been fitted up.

So what next?

Now that I was sure that George wasn't the killer, it was time to start looking for the real culprit. As the residents of Carluke had been asking me for years, I needed to look properly into the case, even if ultimately I might not be able to uncover anything that was new, or significant. However, I knew that at the very least I had to try to get some justice for Margaret – and for George.

*

The policing, investigatory and criminological worlds have changed a great deal since 1973, and I have played a small part in those changes. I've witnessed how these developments can be harnessed to bring perpetrators to justice in live investigations, and how cold cases can suddenly become hot again when the right questions are asked about old evidence.

I wanted to bring my experience of these worlds home to Carluke.

To do so, I first started to concentrate on how Margaret was murdered, and to think about what sort of person might typically kill in this way. I asked myself, what did the crime scene in the glen indicate, and what should we make of how Margaret's body was managed after she had died? What does all of this tell us about what might have motivated the murderer? And, perhaps most importantly of all, could I infer something about the person who would have committed such a murder from the crime scene characteristics that had been reported at the time?

These questions inevitably bring us into territory that is often popularly called 'offender profiling', or 'crime scene analysis', although I tend to describe what I do as falling within 'investigative psychology'.

There is now a reasonably long history of profiling, as the very first 'profiles' were constructed by the FBI in the late 1970s and early 1980s. These have been criticised as being nothing more than 'cold readings' – sophisticated guesswork akin to horoscopes, with no basis in fact – or, more generously, as being based on the personal and professional intuition of the specific profiler. In other words, they lacked any scientific or objective basis. Based on just thirty-six interviews with convicted serial killers and rapists (fictionalised in the Netflix series *Mindhunter*), these profiles were limited in their scope, and based very much on the statements of serial killers during interviews – never the most trustworthy of sources, in my experience. Despite this, it was claimed by the FBI that, based on whether a crime scene was 'organised' or 'disorganised', it would be possible to suggest something about the person carrying out the crime. An organised crime scene was one where the offender had left few clues, because the crime had been carefully planned and was therefore likely to have been committed by someone with an above average IQ, was socially and sexually competent, and probably living with a partner. The organised offender would follow news of the crime in the media and might also leave the area immediately after the commission of the offence.

On the other hand, disorganised crime scenes were originally characterised as ones where there had been little or no attempt to hide any evidence of the crime, were believed to have been committed by someone who lived close to the scene of the offence and who would be socially and sexually inadequate. Often the offender would be living alone, or still living at home with his parents.

We have come to view these early FBI categories of 'organised' and 'disorganised' as much more fluid, with some crime scenes suggesting elements of both, perhaps as a result of the specific circumstances in which the crime was committed. Some of these circumstances would, for example, include how the victim reacted to the attack – such as unexpectedly fighting back, or perhaps the perpetrator being disturbed because the victim screamed, or if he saw members of the public approaching to intervene.

This early form of profiling can provide interesting information, but it needs to be used with some caution. Over time there has been a move away from personal intuition to profiles that are much more evidenced based. I have often characterised this change as moving to profiles that are 'bottom up' and based on the evidence, as opposed to 'top down', which is based on the personal intuition of the profiler.

In this country, especially through the work of Professor David Canter, investigative psychology has become the recognised British approach to profiling. Investigative psychology uses analysis related to three central questions:

1. What happened at the crime scene?
2. What socio-demographic characteristics is the person who carried out the activities observed at the crime scene likely to possess?
3. What are the most likely psychological characteristics of that offender?

This still suggests that the way in which an individual offender carries out a crime is likely to mirror their behaviour in everyday life, but the evidence base for making this suggestion is more robust as it moves beyond the personal, 'top down' insight of the profiler. This approach will also suggest that how the crime was committed will be, at least in part, a reflection of the everyday traits and behaviour of that individual, to the extent that criminal behaviour can mirror other aspects of the offender's daily life.

The early American profiles also discussed motive, even though it is not a legal requirement to establish what the motive might have been for the commission of a crime. Attempting to think about what might have motivated the offender can be a helpful investigatory tool, as in some instances it helps the police to reduce their pool of potential suspects. By motive, we're referring to the emotional, psychological or material needs that first drive the offender and are then satisfied by his offending behaviour. It is not possible to determine what the motive might have been by 'entering the mind' of the offender, even if this is how some of the early American profilers claimed they worked. By using evidence discovered at the crime scene, and through a consideration of which victim had been targeted and how they were then killed, it is possible to suggest something about motivation.

At the start of my own investigation I had to look again at what was reported about how Margaret had been murdered.

The first point to make is that Margaret was 'overkilled'. In other words, her killer inflicted injuries that were far in excess of what was actually needed to cause her death. She received nineteen stab wounds, as well as other injuries – probably punches – to the face. She was stabbed again, and again, and again. This is typical of overkill, which is often perpetrated by people with underlying mental health problems. We should also note that Margaret was not sexually assaulted, nor was her body sexually posed or otherwise 'displayed' after her death. The stab wounds were concentrated on her torso rather than around her sexual organs. The violence used against her was excessive, but non-sexualised, and nor was her body disfigured or mutilated after her death. However, there is no way we can know what the killer might have said when he first encountered Margaret, and it is perfectly possible that the words that he used during the attack were sexualised and demeaning.

Second, the attack does not seem to have lasted for more

than a few minutes. This was a 'blitz' or frenzied attack, which continued until the killer no longer felt the need to go on. Muncie got this aspect of the murder correct. We know that frenzied attacks of this kind are more often than not the result of the offender acting on the basis of cumulative wrongs – real or imagined – from those he encounters within his everyday world. He is retaliating against the victim for perceived insults or injustices for which he feels shame; he is therefore acting in a rage; he is hyper-emotional and out of control – he is emotionally disinhibited and high; and, as he would see it, he is attacking his victim in order to 'save face'. By this I mean that Margaret's death was for him a way that he could regain a sense of who he was and what he deserved by right; it was a way of demonstrating his power and control over her; he was performing masculinity.

As all of this suggests, Margaret's attacker would have known her, perhaps because he was related to her, worked with her, was a neighbour, or she was a former or would-be girlfriend.

We know that Margaret's attacker must have brought a knife to the crime scene. She was not killed by a weapon that he may have found in the glen. The knife that the police discovered was not the murder weapon. Did he bring the knife to the glen because he knew that she would be there and alone at that time, or did he carry a knife about with him more generally? These questions have to be considered within the context of thinking about the crime scene – was it organised or disorganised, or did it have elements of both?

I see both organised and disorganised elements within Margaret's murder. If the crime scene had been completely organised, Margaret's body would have been buried, or hidden in some other way, rather than left in the open (albeit in some undergrowth) where it was quite easily discovered by searching officers. Hiding the body would have allowed the killer greater time to compose himself after the commission of the crime, which, in turn, would have allowed him the opportunity to dispose of any incriminating evidence.

Here we should note that, given the frenzied nature of the attack and the amount of blood that was found on the path and in the glen, Margaret's killer would have been covered in forensic evidence. This is a polite way of saying that both he and his clothes would have been soaked in blood, fibres, skin and hair. As my work with violent offenders has repeatedly shown, he would also have been emotionally disinhibited – excited, perhaps even delirious and lost in the moment. Here again Muncie is correct when he suggests that the killer would have arrived home 'with signs of murder on his person'. Those signs would have been immediately obvious, both physically and emotionally.

Yet no witnesses saw anyone who looked elated, or who might have been acting strangely, and nor did anyone come forward to say that they had seen anyone covered in blood near the crime scene, despite its close proximity to the station and to various houses that bordered the glen.

This implies at least two things.

First, that Margaret's killer was able to quickly leave the scene of the murder and change his clothes without raising suspicion; and, second, he was sufficiently aware that he had to do so if he wanted to avoid detection. No worthwhile forensic evidence was ever found that could be used to definitely prove who had killed Margaret. This implies that her killer was likely to have been of above average IQ. He needed a 'safe place' to come down emotionally after the frenzy of the murder and, in all likelihood, this 'safe place' was close to where the murder happened. His murder may have been committed on the spur of the moment, but this safe space gave him a place to hide and avoid detection after the murder had been committed; it gave him a chance to think about what he had done. The conclusion has to be that he lived in the neighbourhood and in one of the houses close by, as this gave him the necessary sight lines (to Margaret and the glen), easy access to a weapon and a way of exiting the crime scene after the murder had been committed. As far as I am aware, there were no casual workmen in the area, or people who had been temporarily housed in Unitas Crescent.

A generation of research, which has become a sub-discipline of investigative psychology called geo-profiling, shows that most offenders – including violent offenders – don't travel too far to commit their crimes. They offend in places that they know and which are familiar to them; places they can enter and exit with ease, without getting caught. This familiarity of place gives them the confidence to offend, and it is unlikely that they would offend in spaces that they did not know through living or working there.

I think that it is also important to note that there was a limited form of robbery within the murder. The money that Margaret had been given by her mother was stolen, but none of the property in her bags was taken. The ring on her little finger had been removed, although this was later found after the police had cleared and searched the glen, but neither her engagement ring nor a bracelet that she was wearing have ever been recovered. This is significant. Margaret's killer might have taken the bracelet and/or the ring as he intended to sell them – by all accounts, the engagement ring was especially impressive. However, this would run the risk of the ring being identified and the prospective buyer might have alerted the police. The ring would therefore seem more likely to have been removed for expressive and symbolic reasons, rather than the instrumental returns that would have come through selling it on.

It could be, of course, that the engagement ring was better hidden in the undergrowth than Margaret's other ring, and the police simply failed to find it. I have to raise this as a possibility although I strongly doubt it, and believe that the theft of her engagement ring is of great importance. Why?

The engagement ring had been given to Margaret by her fiancé and, as mentioned before, some newspapers reported that she had proudly shown it off around the neighbourhood. It was a symbol of her intended marriage, and that she was involved with someone. This someone was an 'outsider', rather than an inhabitant of Carluke. He was not 'one of us'. Bob was a successful businessman, who had a house in Bearsden and who, on the night that Margaret was murdered, was working in South Africa. Even if these details were only vaguely known, in a small town like Carluke I wonder to what extent these circumstances would have built up jealousy.

It is easy to view the theft of Margaret's engagement ring as a form of 'trophy taking': the ring is a symbol of achievement and victory over Margaret by her killer – and perhaps also of the killer's victory over Bob.

In thinking about her murder more criminologically, we might see Margaret's homicide conforming to what is known as 'anger retaliatory' – a term originally used within a typology of serial rapists. The evidence base for these offences suggests that such crimes are emotional, impulsive and frenzied. Physical behaviour in this type of crime would include ripping the victim's clothing, overkill and the excessive use of force. Typically the attack would be unplanned, but focused on a specific victim who is seen by the offender as the source of his hurt feelings, whether real or imagined. There could also be contributory factors which would have created the circumstances in which this particular offender would want to act against this particular victim; these factors could include mental illness, low self-esteem, stress or drug and alcohol use.

Given that I have mentioned mental illness, it is important to acknowledge that the majority of violent crimes – including murder and homicide – are carried out by people who do not have mental health problems. In fact, people with mental illness are more dangerous to themselves than they are to other people. However, there is a small number of individuals with more serious mental health issues, such as psychosis and personality disorders, who commit acts of violence, especially if they have not been given appropriate help, or if they are abusing alcohol or drugs. Psychosis is characterised by the individual having an impaired relationship with reality; he will often experience hallucinations, or have thoughts which are contrary to actual evidence. Longitudinal studies have shown that, for example, people with schizophrenia or other psychotic disorders who are not receiving treatment are four to seven times more likely to commit a violent crime than the general population.

*

How does all of this allow us to think more broadly about who might have targeted Margaret, or how the police might have gone about investigating the case? In working with hundreds of murderers for nearly forty years I know that murder makes no sense if thought of as only a single act of violence. There is always a context in which that violence is used and, more often than not, the perpetrator has regularly used violence – though perhaps a different form of violence – in the past. The type of attack in which Margaret was killed, a blitz which involved repeated stabbing and had both organised and disorganised elements, would have had some origins within the culprit's life more generally and any previous offending history.

The first point to reinforce is that I have no doubt Margaret would have known her killer. The chances of a random stranger, at that time, also making his way to the station – or at least being in that vicinity – harbouring murderous intentions towards Margaret (or indeed any other woman) and then being able to simply disappear without being spotted or leaving a trace are quite frankly remote, bordering on the impossible. The only sensible conclusion is that Margaret knew her attacker. Door-to-door enquiries in the immediate area would therefore be a good way to begin to sift the pool of potential suspects. In an era before we could simply use Facebook to determine who was in Margaret's circle of friends, it would have been crucial to talk to her family about her wider circle of friends and acquaintances. Nor in 1973 would the police have had mobile phone records to determine whom she might have been speaking to in the hours leading up to her murder. However, they could look into who was in the area at the time that Margaret set off for the station. They could ask witnesses if anyone was seen to be acting suspiciously; if anyone was attempting to sell stolen jewellery;

who was known to carry a knife; or who might have previous convictions for knife crimes. They would need to establish if anyone who lived locally had a history of mental illness or drug addiction, or appeared to be acting strangely around the time of the murder.

And now I had started to do the same, albeit with half a lifetime's gap since the events.

*

More often than not, murder victims know their killer because they are, or have formerly been, in a relationship with them. Husbands kill wives and boyfriends kill girlfriends. We know that Margaret's fiancé was in South Africa at the time of her murder, but that doesn't discount former boyfriends, or young men who might have wanted to have been Margaret's boyfriend. Margaret was described as 'reserved' and 'quiet', which was meant to convey that she had had little sexual experience, but she still had some relationship history. Prior to meeting Bob I had been told that she had been dating a man from Wishaw. Key questions for the police would be: did any of these boyfriends or would-be boyfriends use knives as part of their employment, or perhaps have a history of petty offending? Did they have a history of mental illness, or were they known to be alcoholic, or abuse drugs?

This type of blitz attack doesn't just happen out of the blue, despite what we see on TV crime dramas. It has a context and the perpetrator is likely to have had an offending history and/or to have been hospitalised for underlying mental health problems. He would perhaps have had an inconsistent employment history, or would likely have become known as someone who was unreliable. Perhaps it would be claimed that he had some history of 'illness' – which would have resulted in him finding it difficult to hold down a job, or at least that would be what was said on his behalf. Here we should remember that mental illness, which I have now mentioned several times, would not have been something which was openly discussed in 1973. At that time it would have been seen as shameful, and so disguised as something else or kept secret; hushed up so that the neighbours didn't find out. And again, I must stress that simply because someone has a mental illness it does not mean that they are likely to go on and kill – it's only very specifically in this kind of frenzied attack that we see an increased link to those with certain mental illnesses.

The killer was both organised and disorganised. This implies that he could at times be perfectly capable of living his life like others around him, but there would nonetheless be something about him that gave people who knew him cause for concern. He would be prone to outbursts of temper, or unreasonable and exceptional behaviour. He wouldn't have been trusted by colleagues, friends or family.

One thing that I remain puzzled by was whether the attack was planned or unplanned. Margaret's killer brought the knife to the crime scene and was able to get rid of it later, but the differing reasons for carrying that knife will suggest a competing picture of whether the killer was organised or disorganised. If the killer always carried a knife, or did so because he happened to see Margaret making her way to the station and then found a knife with which to kill her at that time, suggests crime-specific differences in how the killer executed the murder. If the latter, this would mean that he had some way of observing Margaret's movements and knew when she was out alone. Perhaps he stalked her. Perhaps he was watching her all the time, without her realising. Here we need to remember that Margaret could have travelled to Glasgow that night with her sister, and if she had she would in all probability still be alive today. I can see no credible way that the killer knew of her movements in advance. So how was the killer able to observe her? Was he returning home as she was going out? Did he intend to catch the train to Glasgow too?

The more I looked at the case, the more questions I had, and which I needed to answer in order to get a broader picture of the killer's motives – but a picture was forming.

As he woke up that Friday, on the morning of 6 July 1973, I believe that Margaret's killer had no idea that he would end her life that day. However, if my thinking about his motivation is accurate, I believe that he must have harboured a great deal of anger towards her; he was obsessional and his anger – which had perhaps been brewing for some time – spilled over so that, as he saw it, she deserved everything that she had coming to her. This should not be taken to mean that his anger was rational. Far from it. The way that the murder was committed suggests that it was the product of disordered thinking and fantasy. To that end, and for him, in that moment, Margaret's death would have been a righteous slaughter.

In that respect Muncie was wrong – Margaret's death wasn't motiveless at all. It was filled with meaning and significance for the man who killed her, a man who I now firmly believe could not be George Beattie. Killing Margaret allowed the true perpetrator to re-order the world so that he felt less powerless, ashamed and ignored. Perhaps he had always felt like this, and in other aspects of his life too, but there must have been something else about Margaret, something that he had perhaps projected onto her and which she might have been blissfully unaware of, but it had begun to build up inside him until it became a force that he no longer felt able to control.

I mention George because I want to be honest about the fact that he had an inconsistent employment history and that, as someone known as a teller of 'tall tales', he would not have been seen as someone who could be trusted. As I have suggested, all of this means that it would have been important for the police to have interviewed George and rule him in, or out, as a suspect.

But aside from that, the various characteristics of the killer don't actually fit George at all. His inconsistent employment history was undoubtedly the result of his lack of education rather than any underlying clinical problem. Likewise, while he might have had a low IQ and been immature, there is no evidence of mental illness, or drug or alcohol use, nor is there any petty offending in his background. He may have been a bullshitter, but there is no suggestion that he was prone to violent outbursts of temper, or of unreasonable and exceptional behaviour. He had no criminal record, and had never been hospitalised as a result of mental health issues. And while this type of profiling might not have been available to Muncie at the time, it was relatively easy to establish what George's movements were on the night that Margaret was murdered.

Looking beyond George was the investigation that the police should have initiated; these were the circumstances in which they would have had to weigh up the evidence that they could uncover and assess the witnesses, or suspects whom they wanted to interview.

That investigation didn't happen.

As I have alluded to with my mention of Facebook and mobile phone records, policing in 1973 was a very different world from the policing that we have today and, at that time, forensic science was still in its infancy. The first time DNA evidence was used to solve a murder was not until over a decade later, in 1987. I have to be fair in looking at the case with a balanced view and remembering the restrictions on policing at the time, and the then state of forensic science. Muncie had no DNA fingerprinting and only rudimentary forensics to rely on; there was no offender profiling or investigative psychology; nor were police interviews of suspects taped; the Scottish Police as an organisation was also still a hodgepodge of small local and larger regional forces, with tribal loyalties within and between these various groups. In this sense, any investigating I do has some distinct advantages given the development of forensics and criminal psychology over the intervening years.

Frankly, finding the suspect in 1973 did not look promising; to find one within a week was extraordinary.

Given these challenges facing the police, I had to ask how far Muncie had been prepared to go to arrest someone for Margaret's murder. In his handling of this investigation, and in the arrest and charging of George, it becomes very clear how far the cunning old fox was prepared to go – all the way, even if that meant the wrong person was actually arrested.

*

How did Muncie get this so wrong?

Well, first he deployed his unwavering faith in his own

ability to catch the perpetrator and, after settling on a likely suspect, he allowed his confirmation bias to blind him to evidence that demonstrated that he was mistaken. There was no forensic evidence of any kind to link George to the murder – no blood, hair or fibres. There were witnesses who could vouch that George had not been acting unusually at the time of the murder, and on the morning after the murder had been committed, when he was given a lift back from work. However, Muncie wasn't seeking out new information – he was oblivious to anything that pointed in a different direction from George. Rather than change tack, Muncie developed tunnel vision and that became a disease that then infected the rest of the investigation.

It was 'Manuelitis' all over again. Muncie employed strategies which were at best ill-advised, and at worst corrupt, from flying in a newspaper's aeroplane and allowing pictures of the crime scene to be published, despite the fact that at that stage there was still an on-going investigation, to failing to disclose the scientific evidence related to the knife. Not only that, he would then go on to give evidence in court in which he *still* suggested that the knife found in the glen was the murder weapon, even when he knew categorically that it was not.

These are serious charges against a man with a distinguished police career, and I do not make them lightly. Nonetheless, I'm not the first to do so, and I have not gone as far as others in their criticism of Muncie's handling of this case – as any internet search would reveal, and as a 1983 TV documentary about the case argued. It would also be fair to note that Muncie's personal tunnel vision was replicated in other parts of the Scottish criminal justice system – most obviously the procurator fiscal's office and then the appeal court – which were supposed to stand back and reflect on what had happened in Carluke and on the case that Muncie had made against George Beattie. They did not, but rather were simply carried away with this flawed investigation and so the contagion continued to spread.

Frankly, what happened both during the investigation and thereafter cannot be called a search for the truth; the truth was the last thing that was being searched for.

It is hard to escape the conclusion that George was 'fitted up' by Muncie, and then the Scottish criminal justice system simply accepted what had happened as fact. Muncie got promoted to Assistant Chief Constable; George was sent to prison; and everyone else just got on with their lives. However, placing sole responsibility for this miscarriage on the investigating detective, policing more generally or even the legal culture of the time is tempting, but rather too easy. Rather than blaming William Muncie, does Carluke need to look to itself?

That question could only be answered in one place.

It was time to go home, only this time not as a son, or as a brother to wet a newborn's head, or grieve the passing of a loved one, but as a criminologist.

It was time to look at Carluke in a way I'd never done before – as someone who knows all about murder.

CHAPTER FOUR

Carluke: Past and Present, and Introducing the Bake House Café

'Unity, Liberty, Charity'

Perhaps because one of its most famous sons was the founding father of the Ordnance Survey, those few histories of Carluke which exist are always keen to be very specific about where it is situated. For the record, Carluke lies in the heart of the South Lanarkshire countryside, 4.7 miles north-west of Lanark and 4.2 miles south-east of Wishaw. As an ancient royal capital of Scotland, with a statue of William Wallace to boot, I daresay Lanark will be rather better known than Wishaw but, even so, this geographic precision within lowland Scotland and my historical allusion might still not get us too far.

Let's widen the geography a little further to set the scene.

Carluke is often described as a small town situated between Glasgow and Edinburgh. Sadly, whilst accurate, this rather reduces Carluke to what it is not, rather than what it is, although even now most Scots would still see Carluke as simply a stop on the main west coast railway line between Glasgow and Lanark.

Lanark has always been Carluke's smaller but more illustrious neighbour, not only as a result of its historic royal connections, but also because that was where the sheriff court was located, as well as a racecourse, and a livestock market where my father used to buy and sell cattle. It even had a cinema. It wasn't until the building of a trunk road between Glasgow and Carlisle, and then the establishment of Carluke's railway station, prompting a population growth in the nineteenth century, that Carluke seemed to gain some identity and more townsfolk. By the end of the century some four thousand people were living in the town.

The railway has always been important to Carluke's history, its present circumstances and, no doubt, what happens to it in the future. The railway was, of course, also central in Margaret's murder.

With the commercial links that were created by the railway and the trunk road, the town's population not only grew, but prospered. Carluke had a mixed economy of both agriculture and industry. These industries were cotton weaving, and then coal mining, as well as the manufacture of bricks, glass, jam – the town is close to the plentiful fruit farms that grew up beside the River Clyde – and, most delicious of all, confectionery. I remember only too well the hard-boiled minty Carluke Balls which were the source of my childhood dental problems.

Like most Scottish towns there are roads named after local war heroes, with Carluke's three recipients of the Victoria

Cross – William Angus, Thomas Caldwell and Donald Cameron – all having streets named in their honour. To commemorate the centenary of the end of the First World War in 2018, new signs were erected on the main roads coming into town, and also on the platforms at the railway station. These signs proudly proclaim 'Carluke – A Town called Courage'.

The town also has a civic motto: 'Unity, Liberty, Charity'.

As is obvious from this somewhat cursory history, Carluke doesn't really have much to shout about and, when all is said and done, it has become a somewhat anonymous commuter town, where people take advantage of its excellent rail and road links to come and, more often than not, to go again. The fourteen thousand or so who currently make up the town's population are not likely to put down permanent roots, and the majority of the people that I grew up with in the 1960s and early 1970s have moved away. Those residents that have remained tend to be older than the average person now living in the town and will often define Carluke by what no longer exists, but was central to their childhoods.

I'm no different.

The old Rankin library, where I borrowed my first books as a child, has been replaced by a much more modern creation called the South Lanarkshire Lifestyles facility; Carluke High School – the 'big school' – where Margaret, the youngest of my three sisters, was once school captain, has similarly been replaced by something more in keeping with progress. The two local grammar schools have made way for comprehensive education. The High Street, where my family would leave the farm to shop on a Saturday morning, has been pedestrianised, but is largely devoid of actual shops; and the branch of the

Royal Bank of Scotland, where Alison, my eldest sister once worked, long ago closed its doors. Even the tennis club, where I learned all about backhands and forehands, top spin and slice, kick serves, drop shots and volleys has had to make way for new houses.

*

Carluke's other famous son is Dr Daniel Reid Rankin, who worked as a doctor in the town for over fifty years, until his death in 1882. Rankin was one of those eminent Victorians who has now – rather undeservedly – almost disappeared from view. He was an historian, a geologist of some note, and an avid collector of fossils, which meant that he became an early and enthusiastic supporter of Darwin. As such, he acquired a modicum of fame, but his local reputation persists because he was the town's trusted doctor.

The best sources for finding out more about Rankin are the historian Dr Peter J. Gordon and a short biography published by one of his descendants, Daniel Rankin Stuert. Gordon describes Rankin as a 'tall, handsome man, who dressed in a tight-fitting surtout coat, with flowing shirt, tight knee breeches, hessian boots, and a tall silk hat'. Under the hat he hid unfashionably long, reddish hair. Other sources describe him as having a handsome face, 'the brow being high and broad, the eyebrows bushy and fair, the blue eyes big and expressive'. Stuert suggests that Rankin was careless with money, even if he was also the trustee of the local savings bank; a man who disliked sports because of the drinking that was often associated with games; and someone who, after first falling in love but being ultimately rejected, 'never bothered the lassies again'. In fact, the same might be said of why he wore his hair so long. The story goes that he visited a barber just once, but was so disappointed by the results that he refused to return.

Gordon also says that Rankin was 'one of the country's great eccentrics' and it is perhaps this which explains why his fame is only partial. These eccentricities ranged from riding a black horse on visits to his patients and jumping the garden gate or the wall surrounding the house when he arrived, rather than dismounting; walking into the homes of his patients without first knocking on the door, 'as if he was a member of the family'; and, perhaps most eccentric of all, standing on his head to receive people he did not like. Steurt explains how Rankin hated being accosted by people demanding medical advice and, as someone who is stopped in the street for criminological advice, I can sympathise. Steurt describes an incident when Rankin was asked for a medical opinion by one of the townswomen. He had her close her eyes and stick out her tongue. Once she had done so, Rankin simply abandoned her in the street.

In an early version of an opinion about Carluke that has endured to this day, Steurt quotes a number of Rankin's contemporaries who thought it 'a pity that Dr Rankin ever should have been thrown away on a country town', rather than 'being drawn into the great world'. Still, Carluke was and remains proud of its connection with Rankin, demonstrated by the fact that just three years after his death the Rankin Memorial Library and Town Hall was erected by public subscription in his honour. Sadly, when Carluke went through a 'regeneration' programme in the 1980s, these historic buildings were knocked down and replaced with shops and a supermarket, although, in some form of civic compensation, the area is now known as Rankin Gait. It is hard to escape the conclusion that small, lowland 'country towns' were not the types of places where the 'great men' of Scotland were supposed to stay.

*

I have always been an outsider to Carluke. My three sisters all seemed much better at being able to adjust to Carluke's culture after our family moved into the town from our old house in the surrounding countryside. All three of them eventually set up home in Carluke, while I was always off to Glasgow, then to Cambridge and also to New York. They might find this hard to believe, but I rather envied them that adjustment and still marvel at how they negotiated the swings and roundabouts of being the 'clever daughters' of a local farmer who, after the farm had been sold, became the manager of the once-thriving brick factory on Wilton Road, when he wasn't spending time in the Masonic Lodge.

Gender, as ever, played its part in all of this.

Clever girls had limited options, while clever boys had the world at their feet. This wasn't meritocracy; it was prejudice. The horizons of my sisters were dominated by choices that centred on primary school teaching, nursing or clerical work – at least, until they got married and started a family. When I was growing up, our family always seemed to be defined by my father and what he did, rather than by our tireless, astute mother and by her talents and skills.

I worry that I might have unwittingly colluded in this discrimination by not suggesting that my sisters could easily have been running schools, creating education policy, or becoming brain surgeons if they had wanted to. Perhaps that's why, even now, I try to atone by reminding them that they were funnier, faster, cleverer and more gifted than I ever was. But that was not how things turned out. My gender allowed me to move on, while they had to stay. I was permitted – perhaps even expected – to develop a different narrative, whilst they were firmly rooted in one that had been written years before. I wonder how many other Scottish women were shoehorned into this same narrative, with all the damage that would have been done to their own individual aspirations, or indeed the development of Scottish culture as a whole. Perhaps I am not just describing the horizons for women in Scotland, but more broadly.

I should add, I am not suggesting that my life has somehow been 'better' than the lives my sisters have led. Far from it. All that I am trying to convey is that in the culture of my childhood it seemed to me that choices – real, authentic choices – were for the lucky, male few – not for the many. Despite often being told that we could do anything that we wanted, most people just had to get on with things as they were. No questions were asked, because none were necessary.

This is not to say that there weren't women who had choices and made the most of them. One of those was our MP, Judith Hart, who represented the constituency of Lanark (later Clydesdale) from 1959 to 1987. Hart was a major player in Labour politics, and was on the 'hard left' of the party. She supported CND and was on the first Aldermaston march in 1958; she favoured nationalisation and public sector job creation; she campaigned against corporal punishment in schools; and fought poverty and injustice at home and abroad.

I remember her knocking on our door on several occasions,

and what struck me was, first, how flamboyant and stylish she was, and then how, over a cup of tea, she would argue with genuine passion for my parents' and my sisters' votes. She was exceptional. When she was elected in 1959, she was one of only twenty-five women MPs (another entering the House of Commons for the first time that year was Margaret Thatcher); she was only the fifth woman to serve in the Cabinet; and, for much of the 1980s she was the only female Scottish MP.

Perhaps above all else, what Judith Hart's extraordinary career reveals is that she bucked the trend of the gender discrimination that existed at this time, and therefore just how difficult it really was for my sisters and their friends to choose lives less ordinary for themselves.

I cannot deny that I had advantages through the choices that were mine, including the choice to move away from Carluke. Being in education for as long as I was meant that I did not have to find a job until well into my twenties. By the same age my sisters were all firmly embedded in their careers and Margaret and Annie had already started families. So too I met people that I would never have encountered had I not had those choices; individuals who were different from me, and who wanted to celebrate those differences. Many of these people are still my friends. The uniform and inclusive, close-knit culture of Carluke might have offered high employment, job security, a sense of community and a clear, personal narrative, albeit punctuated by class, gender and religious bias, but I found that it was also constraining and paled to a distant memory in the glorious chaotic, multi-culture of New York in the mid and late 1970s.

*

The inclusive culture of Carluke would disappear during the period of history that social scientists like to call 'late modernity', to be replaced with something much more 'exclusive'.

The criminologist Jock Young has suggested that this 'exclusive society' has, on a national level, spawned economic and social insecurity. This in turn resulted in the increasing fragmentation of personal and social identities and an unwillingness to accommodate immigrants, or those who were seen to be different. What this meant at the micro level – in other words, what it means for a place such as Carluke – is that people were increasingly being employed in the secondary, rather than the primary (often nationalised) labour market, and, more often than not, engaged on short-term contracts. In turn, this created a large swathe of people who have since become viewed as constituting an 'underclass'. This is an ugly, disrespectful term for millions of largely working class white men, who are in reality unemployed, or working for wages that cannot easily sustain family life. Excluded from the labour market, this 'underclass' soon became excluded from civil society and were left stranded in sink estates, where alcoholism, self-harm, suicide and crime are often rife.

When I walk along Carluke's High Street, I see this change over my lifetime. A move from an inclusive society to one that is exclusive. Not only that, but all the empty shops and the charity and betting shops which now dominate the streets of Carluke are merely the outward signs of the more widespread job insecurity and poverty wages that characterise the labour markets of central Scotland. The sources of actual wealth now seem almost invisible.

And it's not just there. For Carluke, substitute the name

of most small towns not just across Scotland but the whole of the UK.

Is the solution to move away?

Well, perhaps, but where would you move to? The reach of late modernity and the breadth of the exclusive society doesn't stop at the Scottish borders, or indeed at the English Channel. The exclusive society is global and will only change when we begin once again to regulate the movement of capital, as we did during the 1960s and 1970s, and also when communities have a collective culture that allows them to challenge what they know to be wrong by uniting together, or at the very least exercising their right to vote. Perhaps for change to happen we need to see things as they really are, rather than viewing them from the perspective of how a small minority of others would like them to be seen.

Fat chance.

Perhaps I'm being too cynical, and I do wonder to what extent this move from an inclusive to an exclusive society might also have prompted some unexpected social, cultural and political changes. Perhaps the full economy of the inclusive society blinded everyone to the reality that the vast majority of people were still working for an elite minority – the minority who owned the brickworks and the mines, the factories and the banks. Did we convince ourselves that we were acting in our own interests, when in fact we were acting in the interests of just a few? Or perhaps we always knew that that was the case, but simply turned a blind eye to that reality. That fiction we've constructed is much harder to ignore when we can see with our own eyes all the closed shops, the charity shops and the obscenity of gross income inequality living cheek by jowl with food banks and the homeless sleeping in doorways.

This reality is even more worrying. It is now so widespread and visible that we realise that it might just threaten us, and our families too.

Carluke, it seems to me, did once believe in this economic fiction, as did many other towns and cities. This fiction shaped the culture of the town – not just an economic culture, but also the social and traditional fabric of how lives were led – and what expectations were then placed on those people's lives. Perhaps the town also believed in a fiction about the criminal justice system; a fiction that such a system would deliver – well, justice. And that's why I feel that it is vital to look into the murder of Margaret McLaughlin and the wrongful conviction of George Beattie.

Perhaps what I have described is too optimistic, but for what it's worth – and here's the irony that still drives me onwards, professionally and as an individual – I am always drawn back.

For all these personal advantages that I have acknowledged and described, many of which came as a result of my moving away, it is to Carluke – whether inclusive or exclusive – that I always want to return. While I still do visit Cambridge, Glasgow and even New York, there is always something that inexorably draws me back to my home town. No matter if I tried, I know that I cannot leave it and nor do I want to.

This is not a past that I am trying to escape from.

Ultimately, family commitments aside, I think that this compulsion to return has to do with the fact that it was the Carluke of my youth that did so much to shape my personal, political and professional life, and which continues to make me who I am today. To go back is to meet myself again. After all, it was my sisters and their friends who showed me what feminism was really all about and what family and community could be like; it was Judith Hart who taught me about politics and how to fight injustice; and it was Carluke that gave me my first ever lessons in the pernicious cultures of silence and denial.

Above all, it was Carluke which first taught me about murder.

It was time for me to go back again and this time to report on what I saw.

*

Carluke is now a commuter town, with its residents coming and going. But this does not stretch to catering for visitors. There are no longer any hotels in the town and precious few restaurants, with only a few takeaways and, for those in the know, the Bake House Café. Retreating Highlanders, whom Dr Rankin described in his overly long (and at times rather boring) history of the town as once having stayed in Carluke in 1745, would find it difficult to find a place to rest for the night these days. As a result, modern tourists make for the utopian socialist village of New Lanark, a World Heritage Site with a splendid hotel, where my nephew Alan works, or, until recently – because on my most recent visit I noted that it has now closed down – the Cartland Bridge Hotel where Paul, another of my nephews, got married. If tourists pass through Carluke at all, they are unlikely to linger. To be fair, there's not much to see.

Of course there are continuities as well as changes.

The Masonic Lodge still stands proudly near one corner of

the Market Square, a reminder that there were once divisions in the town based on religion, as there were in every Scottish town and city. The Wee Thackit Inn stands at another corner. The Wee Thackit's robust, Spartan concrete toilets, and their accompanying pungent aroma, also remind me that not everything benefits from refusing to surrender to progress.

The Market Square still has benches, civic greenery and a fir tree is placed there at Christmas, around which everyone, or at least those who can be bothered to leave the Wee Thackit, will sing carols on Christmas Eve. The square now also has a sign devoted to 'Carluke – Our People', which mentions individuals who are supposedly connected with the town. Inevitably it lists William Wallace, Robert Bruce, Major-General William Roy, Dr Rankin and the three VCs. More interestingly, it also says that 'recent history has seen Carluke being home to some famous men of sport and industry including Dougie Arnott (Motherwell FC), Joe Jordan (Manchester United FC) and Joe Dodds (Celtic FC). The inventor of Slush Puppies previously resided on West Avenue.' West Avenue is the most sought after street in the town.

This latter association does seem to be rather clutching at straws. Indeed, when I read the obituaries of Will Radcliff, the inventor of the Slush Puppie – the syrupy, frozen drink that turns the tongue temporarily blue – who died in 2014, all of them stated that he had been born in Dayton, Kentucky and grew up in Cincinnati, where he invented the drink on his front porch in the early 1970s. I could find no mention of Carluke.

On my first open research visit in January 2017, I walked once again through Rankin Gait with my sisters Margaret and

Alison, and into the High Street where the contrast between the Carluke of my childhood and today was immediately obvious. Of course there were changes that I had known about and had seen before, but returning now with a criminological eye threw them into stark relief. The old toy shop, where my parents had bought me my first tennis racquet, had disappeared to make way for a greetings card shop and, on the opposite side of the street, there was now a food bank.

'A sign of the times?' I suggested to Alison, gesturing to the food bank.

She nodded and mumbled, 'You used to be able to get anything in Carluke, but not now. It's all so depressed.'

The Black Bull Inn, perhaps the oldest building in the town, had closed its doors and looked a shadow of its former rowdy, boisterous self, and R & J Templeton, the independent supermarket where we had done our weekly food shop, has been replaced by Scotmid, a Scottish food chain. Walking on, I encountered a Chinese takeaway and even a Turkish barber shop, which seemed to suggest diversity, but almost immediately I also passed – within a hundred yards of each other, and on the same side of the street – three betting shops, which I'm certain would not have found favour with Dr Rankin.

At the top of the High Street the sweet shop which had done so much to damage my youthful teeth and Coia's café had both closed down.

'Where do you shop now?' I asked Alison.

'The internet,' she replied. Clearly Scotmid was not to her liking.

We were slowly making our way to the Bake House Café in Clyde Street. This is where my sisters meet up with their friends to discuss their lives and make sense of their world, and they were taking me there because they thought that it would also be an ideal place to discuss the murder of Margaret McLaughlin.

They were right, and the women that I met there would become a 'sounding board' with whom I could discuss my research. They would often prompt me to think again, or to think differently, about the various issues that cropped up in what I had discovered.

*

The Bake House Café was opened in 2009 by Laura Allan (now McConnell), who did indeed go off to Motherwell Technical College after the summer holidays had ended in 1973. Throughout my research visits to the town, the café was always warm and welcoming; it was a place that I came to see as safe, solid. For me it has an air of both the confessional booth and the therapist's couch. It has a sense of history too, and pictures of Carluke's three VCs adorn the walls. That makes it sound like a museum and so, just to be clear, and much more importantly, it serves great coffee and all the food that it sells is made on the premises. From the outside the café appears cosy and is often described as such, even though it is large enough to seat up to forty people on the comfy chairs that are dotted about here and there. Perhaps every small town has its own Bake House Café, which acts as an informal social centre; a place where people come to talk about what is happening with their lives and to reach out for human contact; a place to remember, share and plan. If they don't, they should.

If I was writing a novel, at this point in my narrative you would expect me to discuss Laura's age and provide you with a physical description. You would want to know what Laura looks like, and if her looks had faded as she had grown older and when her hair inevitably changed colour. Are her eyes blue or green? Is she slim and petite, or carrying weight that she worries about? You would want to know what secrets she might have hidden and which still lie buried from her past. You would also convince yourself that you just want to know these largely physical details to form a picture in your mind of who 'Laura Allan' is and perhaps to help you differentiate her from the other women that I am going to introduce you to. But I am not writing a novel, and so l am therefore going to deny you these details. I don't want to define these women by what they look like, but instead by their individual qualities as people, and then dazzle you with the force of their person-alities. I don't want to discuss their ages, or their trials and tribulations, but instead allow you to get to know them by the enduring aspects of their beings and humanity that serve to make them who they are.

Instead, let me say that Laura Allan is a woman with a restless energy that perhaps stems from her faith; she fizzes and pops with ideas and plans, and she gives the impression of being able to do anything that she sets her mind to. Even so, she admits that sometimes it has been a struggle to keep the café going, but she has done so almost as a tribute to her grandmother, who she describes as having been a 'coffee-shop person'. She would later joke with me that she had secretly wanted to open a wine shop, but that she was worried that she would drink all of the profits. She was clearly joking, but I teased her and suggested that perhaps it was just as well that she hadn't become an air stewardess! Nor have I ever told her that it is obvious that the Bake House Café really would be a great place to have a glass of wine, or a wee whisky.

On that first research visit I met the women who, along with Laura and my sisters, would form my Bake House Café sounding board.

Despite all of her training in Colonel's Glen, Margo Smith came second in the hundred metres at the Carluke Highland Games in 1973. I get the impression that she's still not happy with the result but, like many Scottish women of her age she put the disappointment behind her and has just got on with life. She gave up running a long time ago, but she still looks fit and keeps herself active. She quickly filled me in with some details about her life. She married a former school friend called David Morrow, and thereafter spent her professional life working in mental health services. She is pragmatic, reflective, and carefully measures her answers to my questions. She has retired, but her grandchildren keep her active.

The other woman who joined us was Maureen Dickson (née Weston), who remembered George Beattie at the wee school and went on to work in the town's post office. Some years after she had married, Maureen would come to live next door to George's mother. Maureen is a good friend of my sister Margaret, and their close friendship meant that it was very easy for her to see me as simply Maggie's brother, as opposed to being a criminologist conducting research. And, like my sister, she's very practical and down to earth, and so speaks her mind without fear or favour. She is also blessed with a good memory – which, I'd soon discover, was not universally shared. More than once it would be Maureen who'd gently correct a stray 'fact' and then marshal it back into the correct time frame.

Bless her, it was my eldest sister, Alison, who was the main offender as far as memory was concerned. Over the course of my research it was typical of her to phone me up the day after one of my visits to the town 'just for a chat'. That chat would invariably include something that she wanted to correct from our earlier discussion. She'd giggle as she did so and then remind me, 'Well, I am getting old, you know!'

In total, I visited the Bake House Café on ten occasions – sometimes to meet the entire sounding board, but at other times just to have a coffee with one or other of my sisters, or to meet up with whoever else might be available. I'd also keep in touch by telephone and email, although I much preferred to sit down in the café, get out my notebook and start jotting down what everyone was saying. As best as I could, I'd take verbatim notes of what we discussed, although at times – especially if they spoke all at once – I'd have to ask someone to repeat what they had just said. On one or two occasions Alison would look at me blankly when I did this, and it would fall to one of the others to reply on her behalf. She didn't seem to object.

All of these women knew the case intimately. Margo and Laura had grown up in Unitas Crescent and could take me back to life in the streets around the railway station before and after the murder. Laura's father had given George a lift back from his work to Carluke on the morning after the murder. Maureen had been at school with George and would later live beside his mother in the town. My youngest sister, Margaret, felt particularly close to the case, as she was a good friend of George's brother John. She never, ever accepted that George was guilty. Margaret is no one's fool, and her support for George had nothing to do with emotion. Over the course of her nursing career she would finally end up in charge of a busy A&E department at a hospital on the outskirts of Glasgow. She knows all about the extremes of existence and survival, and what one human being can do to themselves, or to other people. No, her support for George wasn't about loyalty or sentiment.

These women would help me to understand what happened to Margaret McLaughlin and, thereafter, to George Beattie. They became the heat that brought this cold case back to life and, in the absence of any surviving forensic evidence or access to any relevant legal files, provided a way of getting to understand the case without having to rely on newspaper reports – which was how I had first tried to make sense of the murder. This was sometimes crime-specific but, more often than not, it was about the social and cultural context in which the murder had been committed. Their assistance was to remember Carluke as it was actually lived and experienced in the 1970s, as opposed to the Carluke that has become preserved and presented on the civic statues that populate the Market Square. It was this sounding board that helped me to understand the part played in the murder, and what subsequently happened to George, by deference, class, silence and gender.

Even on that very first visit to the café, in response to some of my broad and opening questions, I started to see another narrative, one different from that which had been presented in the press. Maureen remembered that, back in those days, 'you accepted what the police said; you trusted them. So if they said that's what happened, well, that's what had happened.' Laura and Margo nodded in agreement and Laura added that while she had been acutely aware that what was happening was wrong, she 'wasn't vocal about any of that' – at least not in public.

They told me that, behind closed doors, people were talking about the murder and their disquiet about George's arrest, and were clearly upset when he was later convicted. Margo thought that 'George had been taken advantage of by the police; he was just a convenient scapegoat'. They described how many of the women in the street were suggesting that there was a man 'who was a much more likely suspect' than George. Indeed it was this historical, shared concern that had initially encouraged Maureen, Margo and Laura to agree to contribute to my research when they had been asked to help me by my sisters. As Laura put it to me, she 'liked the idea of solving a mystery and even now getting justice for George'. She also thought that it would be 'cathartic' for the community. She remembered her father William saying that George had only been arrested because 'Muncie wanted to close the case before he retired'. And so, for her, 'this was as much about Muncie as it was about Margaret'.

I would later come to place great importance on William Allan's knowledge about George, and his views about why he had been arrested, especially as it had been William who had given him a lift back to Carluke at such a critical point in the murder timeframe.

After this first session, I took some time to reflect on what I had written down. I was intrigued that both Laura and Margo described how 'most of the women in the crescent' thought that someone else had committed the murder and were openly naming other suspects at the time. I will leave to one side their naming of these other suspects for the moment, but want to note the gendered dimension to what Laura and Margo said: it was 'most of the women in the crescent' who believed in George's innocence. This implies a number of things and also poses an obvious question. Were the women less accepting than the men in the town of the police's version of events? If so, was it perhaps a manifestation of empathy with George that male townsfolk found more difficult to express?

Whatever the answer to this question might be, in 1973 none of us really knew how to go about making public any private disquiet, and so our inability to challenge what was happening to George remained very troubling and confusing. In today's social-scientific jargon, no one felt that they had a 'voice' to contest the status quo. I genuinely felt that something terrible had happened and wanted to know how to put it right. I didn't want to be silent and accepting, and to keep what I felt private or hidden. For me, these problems were alleviated by going off to school and then on to university. In this way I could put a distance between my feelings and what had happened in Carluke. In truth, though, it was never really far from my memory; my awareness that a wrongful conviction might have taken place was almost like a guilty secret.

Like all guilty secrets, it would find ways of making itself public, periodically bubbling to the surface. What happened to George remained as real as ever, and still as perplexing. Even so, I simply accepted the status quo. However, as all of my discussions in the Bake House Café would prove, if they sometimes bubbled to the surface for me, they did so much more powerfully for other people – especially those people who stayed in the town. New appeals brought the case back into public discussions, with every fresh piece of evidence closely re-considered. I hoped from afar that George might one day win his appeal, but he never did and so remained in prison. The same questions would then resurface. How could we all go on living our lives knowing but seemingly not knowing? How could we continue being in denial about what had happened, and that the wrong man had been convicted? On a practical level, how might we mount a challenge to authority, and in what circumstances? If I were to do so, would that impact on my own life, or the lives of my family, if I was seen to make too many waves?

Today, I would know how to begin to answer some of these questions. My professional life is often peppered with the moral dilemmas that crop up when working with offenders and that grey area that all too often exists between the certainties of the black and the white. Should prison be about punishment or rehabilitation? Which offenders should be offered parole and who should be denied? Are young children who commit crime responsible for their actions? My general views on these issues, and about specific cases, have sometimes made me unpopular. I've also had to learn how to create a balance between the professional and the personal, juggling the demands of being a husband and a father with knowing when to speak publicly about an unpopular truth.

But the questions that cropped up in the Bake House Café and the steps towards answering them were not from the present; they were from the past. Trying to answer them honestly was therefore going to be an exercise in raising ghosts; ghosts which I felt that I had long since exorcised. However, as I was soon to discover, I wasn't just visiting the Carluke of the here and now as the person that I have become, but immersing myself once more in the Carluke of my childhood, with all of its hopes, dreams, ambitions, disappointments and regrets.

A Carluke where a murder had just been committed and the real culprit had been allowed to evade justice.

CHAPTER FIVE

Cultures of Silence and Denial

'We Will Pay You $4.00 for One Hour of Your Time. Persons Needed for A Study of Memory'

T he dinner table of my childhood was rectangular, made of a solid, dark wood, and could comfortably sit eight people. Most of the time it was covered with a plastic sheet, but this would be removed and replaced with a white linen tablecloth if visitors came to join us for supper. All of our meals were taken around this table and I remember that we rather envied our friends who were allowed to eat in front of the TV, watching their favourite programmes, avoiding having to make conversation with their parents and siblings. Silence was a luxury in our house, where we were expected to have an opinion about local, national or world events.

Looking back, I now realise that most of the time my opinions were based on disagreeing with anything that my father said. I started to worry that this personal archaeology, which was a necessary component of my research, might provide me with glimpses of other unsettling realities about my parents, and about me as a child.

In the summer of 1973 discussions around the dinner table were taken up by the murder of Margaret and the conviction of George Beattie.

I got the distinct impression that my dad knew Muncie well, but not that they were close friends. Muncie certainly never visited our house and I don't recall my father discussing visiting his. Now I wonder if they had perhaps attended the same Masonic Lodge, although I simply don't know – I was never a Mason myself. For whatever reason, they were aware of each other and Muncie's name cropped up several times, especially in relation to family discussions about the crimes committed by Peter Manuel. In that respect Muncie was rightly regarded by my father as someone who was professional in his approach, and who had done an especially good job in bringing Manuel to justice.

For that reason, the Manuel investigation coloured his thinking about the murder of Margaret McLaughlin and the conviction of George Beattie.

The essence of my father's point of view was that the 'police know what they're doing' and that a jury had found their case convincing enough to have convicted George of Margaret's murder. The gossip in the town as to the identity of a much more likely suspect – as others might have seen things – was to be ignored.

End of story.

Of course I now realise that it is possible to take a more cynical view of my father's stance. Challenging the police's version of events might lead to issues and problems that my father would have then had to manage in Carluke, but these could be avoided by accepting their account of the murder. Had the Lodge perhaps created loyalties that transcended the truth? I remember an old saying from the time that the Lanarkshire police were just 'the Masonic Lodge with truncheons'.

At the time I found my father's certainty unsatisfying, confusing and hypocritical. As children we had been taught by our parents to be respectful of other people's feelings and, obviously, never to hurt them either physically or emotionally. We had also been taught to be respectful to people in authority. I couldn't determine which lesson had the greater force if it was someone in authority that we believed was causing the harm. If my sisters were right, wasn't it Muncie – Scotland's 'top detective' – who was in the wrong, and if that was the case, shouldn't we be saying that? Did we not have a moral responsibility to challenge what had happened? I can't pretend that I was able to answer this conundrum at the time and there was little that I could do, except to keep raising it when the occasion demanded. That occasion seemed to present itself every time we sat down to eat.

In 1973 two of my sisters were still living at home. Alison had returned home after giving up on nursing. As she explained to our parents, she hated the hierarchy that existed in nursing at that time, and had been unable to reconcile her personal and political views with that hierarchy. Alison was always a rebel. She wore long hippy skirts, dyed her hair in vivid colours and would go off to England to attend rock concerts – coming back home with stories of a world beyond Carluke, Scotland and indeed Britain. She tried to convince

Annie and Margaret that nursing might not suit them either, but her advice fell on deaf ears. Annie ploughed her own furrow and had married the previous year, in July 1972, and was living with her husband on the other side of Carluke. She would become a very successful midwife, delivering babies throughout the county before she finally retired. Margaret was the youngest of my three sisters and the closest in age to me. However, we didn't go to the same school, had different interests – especially our taste in music – and it was only as adults that we became friends, as opposed to brother and sister. She knew George's brother John Beattie and so occasionally, especially as I grew older, I would hear stories about how George was doing in prison and of the various twists and turns of his latest appeal. Margaret has never at any point accepted that George was guilty and she and her friends always believed that he was being 'scapegoated', or as she put it to me recently, 'He was being used by the police. They just wanted a conviction. No one that I knew thought he was guilty.'

Given the strength of Margaret's views, even years later we had to be tactful about raising this subject around the dinner table with our parents.

In between the discovery of Margaret McLaughlin's body and the arrest of George, my father had taken to driving my sisters about town, rather than allowing them to walk or cycle. My mother had been particularly worried that a killer was on the loose. I'm sure much the same thing was happening in households all over Carluke. A sense of fear gripped the town, and though the time between the murder and arrest was short, it took months for things to return to normal, only really coming back to some semblance of familiarity after George's conviction.

That sense that life could return to normal after George's conviction seemed absurd to me. We all felt that he was innocent, so what about the real killer? Even if my father agreed with George's conviction (or at least said that he did) my sisters and their friends thought that the wrong man had been found guilty, and so the real killer was still at large. What if he was to strike again? As it happened, no further murders occurred in Carluke until many years afterwards, but there had been no guarantees that this would be the case. And, of course, life would never return to normal for the McLaughlins.

But why did we all simply allow our disquiet about what was happening to remain a topic of dinnertime conversation, as opposed to prompting us to take action? Why were these discussions taking place behind closed doors, rather than being shouted from the rooftops? Why did people defer to the police's version of events?

A book first published in 1974 might just hold some of the answers.

*

The place to start is in trying to understand why people defer to those with power, and how that deference weaves its way into the fabric of all of our lives, which, in turn, limits an individual's ability to take action. Freedom to take action – to have the free will to do so – is accepted as a fundamental and universal element of what it means to be human. In the social sciences, the capacity of an individual to be independent in this way and to have the capacity to act so as to influence the course of events that shape their life is described as having 'agency'. But to what extent is agency constrained by the societal structures of gender, class or ethnicity, and, more broadly, of power? These issues bring us face to face with the results of one of the greatest experiments in all of social psychology.

Stanley Milgram's book *Obedience to Authority: An Experimental View* was published in 1974, the year after Margaret was murdered, but the experiments that formed the basis of that book began in the autumn of 1960. At the time, Milgram ran a class at Yale University called 'The Psychology of Small Groups', and what would later become known as the 'obedience to authority' studies was initially a class experiment involving students. This class then enabled him to broaden his research and put adverts in the local newspapers asking for volunteers from the local community: 'We Will Pay You $4.00 for One Hour of Your Time. Persons Needed for A Study of Memory'.

It was, however, not a study of memory at all, and this subterfuge would be the beginning of criticisms about the design of Milgram's experiment which have endured over time, and still crop up even today.

Milgram's experiment involved a hoax. A white-coated experimenter would take charge of two volunteers, one of whom would be given the role of 'learner' and the other the role of 'teacher'. In the original experiments this learner was not a volunteer at all, but a mild-mannered forty-seven-year-old accountant who had been trained to play the role. As such, he was strapped to a chair and told that he had to remember lists of word pairs. If he was unable to recall these word pairs, the teacher was asked to give him an electric shock. Unbeknown to the teacher, no electric shock was administered and the learner merely acted as if he was being shocked. With each incorrect answer the voltage would increase, with the learner moving from emitting small groans to screams of absolute agony – the mild-mannered accountant was a very good actor. The mechanism for administering these shocks had thirty levels or settings, ranging from 15 volts, which was marked 'slight shock', to 450 volts, which was ominously marked 'XXX'.

The purpose of the experiment was to observe the teacher administering the shocks and see how far they would be prepared to go. Would they obey authority, even in the face of individual suffering?

Astonishingly, over 60 per cent of the teachers were prepared to administer shocks at the level of 'XXX', despite the apparent agony and pain of the learner.

What Milgram's experiment showed was that when people are faced with *doing good* in support of a fellow human being or *being good* in doing as they were told, they would opt for the latter.

In the Carluke case, George was the learner who couldn't remember a simple word pair, and therefore deserved what he got. He was a teller of tall tales, had learning difficulties and was seen by some as being odd. These personality traits might have, for some, devalued George's status as an individual and made it easier to accept that he should be punished. If people in Carluke – people like my father – accepted that the police were the professionals, the experts in the understanding of crime and offenders, then what right had mere members of the public to challenge their authority? They must know what they are doing and, the belief ran, the whole criminal justice system was set up to protect the public and was therefore worth supporting. It is easier to ignore the rights of one individual who might have been unfairly treated if it is to ensure the sanctity and continuance of a greater, worthier cause. The cognitive dissonance in challenging authority would, especially at that time, have caused a great leap into the unknown. Rumours and gossip were all well and good, but acting on them and disrupting the status quo was out of the question. Instead we were encouraged to focus on the technicalities of the appeals process within the Scottish criminal justice system and hope that their strange logic and procedural rules might eventually deliver the truth.

Just as well we didn't hold our breath.

*

Here's another experiment to consider. Imagine that you are in a public room of a hotel when, slowly at first, your surroundings start to fill with smoke. Quite quickly it becomes obvious that there is a problem. How long would it take you to go and seek help? Would you look to other people in the room to see whether you should? This scenario is the basis of a famous experiment that was used to help to understand 'bystander apathy' – people not coming to the aid of those who need help.

In the experiment, individuals were asked to fill in a questionnaire measuring their attitudes towards 'urban life' and were taken to a room to complete the survey. Depending on the specific scenario, the participant could either be in the room alone, with two strangers, or with two people who, unbeknownst to the participant, were actually part of the experiment. After a short time, smoke would be pumped into the room and then the reactions of the participants were noted.

These results are again of great relevance to themes at the heart of this story – perhaps all the more so as the experiments were designed in part to explain the circumstances surrounding the murder of a young woman called Kitty Genovese in New York in March 1964.

When the participants were alone, 50 per cent had left the room to seek help within two minutes of the smoke first appearing, and after six minutes 75 per cent of them had left. If there were two other strangers in the room, only 12 per cent had left the room after two minutes and, after six minutes, the numbers of participants leaving had increased to 36 per cent – a rise, but hardly a significant one. However, if the participant was in the room with the two people who were part of the experiment, who had been instructed to act as if nothing was wrong, only 10 per cent of the participants *ever* left the room, even when the smoke became so dense that the participant wouldn't have been able to see their questionnaire. In other words, what this experiment showed is that the presence of other people inhibits individuals from responding to an emergency situation, especially if those other people don't respond to the situation as if it was an emergency.

A couple of phrases aptly capture what lies behind these results: 'diffusion of responsibility' and 'pluralistic ignorance'. How exactly does pluralistic ignorance and diffusion of responsibility help us to make sense of what might happen in the real world, as well as in the smoke-filled rooms of a social experiment?

Pluralistic ignorance simply means that, in the scenario

where the two people act as if nothing is wrong, the bystander doesn't react to the smoke entering the room as an emergency because he or she believes that no one else is concerned. Even if the bystander did decide that something was wrong, he or she would then have to decide if they were going to take personal responsibility to try to rectify that situation. Other people in the room inhibit that decision because their presence leads to a diffusion of responsibility: a sense of personal responsibility decreases as the number of other people grows.

The importance of noticing that an emergency is taking place and interpreting that event as an emergency and then assuming personal responsibility to rectify that situation, are the first three phases of a five-phase cognitive model of 'helping behaviour' – the opposite of bystander apathy. The final two phases would be an awareness of what the appropriate form of assistance would be (for example, knowing the number for the police) and, finally, implementing the decision to help (dialling that number).

Helping behaviour is actually difficult to define. There is a world of difference between an assistant in a shop who offers to help you and someone who rushes into a burning building to save the occupants who are trapped inside, even if both are examples of helping behaviours. In the first instance the person is being paid to help, while in the second scenario the individual is displaying a very different form of conduct. We do not need to become entangled in the debate about whether pure altruism exists to see that there is a continuum of helping behaviour which might, at one end, be planned (such as the example of the shop assistant) and, at the other, be spontaneous. Does an individual behave in this latter way without consideration of the benefit that may come to him/ herself, or is this behaviour a means by which that individual overcomes personal distress? Similarly, we might see a difference between direct helping behaviour, such as rushing into the burning building, and indirect behaviour which might, for example, simply involve calling 999.

Before considering how all of this might help us to understand what happened in Carluke, there is one final contribution – this time by a criminologist, rather than a social psychologist – that is worth considering, especially as his ideas allow us to move away from individual motivation and denial, and back to the collective.

*

Professor Stan Cohen was a South African-born academic who had a lifelong interest in human rights and emotional management. He is perhaps best known for developing the concept of 'moral panic', but he also studied how prisoners serving life sentences at HMP Durham could preserve their identity and resist physical and mental deterioration.

In his final book, *States of Denial: Knowing About Atrocities and Suffering*, Cohen asserted that there were three states of denial: literal, interpretive and implicatory denial.

Literal denial asserts that something did not happen, or is not true, and might also be called factual or blatant denial.

On the other hand, interpretive denial accepts the basic facts but a different interpretation is given to them, so that another meaning emerges, despite what others might have claimed. This is not, as with literal denial, a claim that nothing happened, but rather a suggestion that what happened is not what it might look like to other people.

Finally, implicatory denial does not attempt to deny the facts, but rather what is denied is the psychological, political or moral implications that conventionally follow from an acceptance of those facts. Cohen argues that our awareness of the homeless on the streets does not seem to have prompted us to act to prevent this state of affairs from occurring; the awareness does not carry with it, in other words, either a psychological or moral imperative for change. There is no direct refusal to acknowledge the reality of homelessness, but the significance of there being homeless people is minimised, or denied, and so the status quo is preserved. In short, people come to live with suffering.

For Cohen, denial can be personal and individual, private and psychological, or it can be shared and therefore be social and collective. It can also be organised and formalised, so that denial seeps into the structures of institutions and culture more generally. He concludes that 'a deep shame of passivity' should become the mobilising norm of social life.

Cohen's work on denial is thoughtful, challenging and helpful when thinking about the wrongful conviction of George Beattie and the murder of Margaret McLaughlin, largely because he sees denial as both personal and social: his ideas can accommodate both the individual and the broader community in which that individual resides. The obvious temptation is to see George's conviction as a form of implicatory denial, which allowed Carluke to turn a blind eye to what had happened. At this social and collective level I think that this does help to explain what occurred. As such, an awareness of a wrongful conviction did not carry with it a moral imperative to take action to right that wrongful conviction, in much the same way that an awareness of homelessness might make us feel uncomfortable, but does not lead to us taking action to end homelessness.

In my mind, this implicatory denial first emerged and then seeped into individual consciousness, and it was this which allowed different people to collude in a miscarriage of justice. Understanding things in the context of these studies allows us to account for different, individual reactions, rather than totalising how people might have responded. Indeed, all of the research that I have cited appears static – it suggests that people develop a view about an event and that they retain that view thereafter.

Life is much more complicated than that, and certainly more complicated in the Carluke case.

*

Let's start with the obvious point.

What happened in Carluke cannot be explained as pluralistic ignorance. This simply does not work on a number of levels, but at its most basic it does not work as people in the town were not ignorant of suspicions surrounding George's conviction. Indeed, it has been at the encouragement of people in the town that I have embarked on this journey at all, as well as my own anxieties about the case. It has not just been my anxiety which generated a desire to try to work out who had actually killed Margaret McLaughlin, but a disquiet that was shared much more widely. My discussions in the Bake House Café are testament to that, as well as the various emails that I received after I had made it public that I was researching the case. It is impossible to tell exactly how wide this unease might still go, but different people at different times, and mostly independent of one another, raised concerns about George Beattie's conviction.

What I cannot determine with any certainty is if this anxiety occurred immediately, like my own and that of my sisters and some of their friends, or over time, as people had an opportunity to think about what had happened and were then able to come to their own conclusions when more facts were made public. And how long is 'over time'? A few days, a few months, or are we talking about years? This thought made me remember something that had come up in one of our discussions at the Bake House Café. Maureen told me that 'the more I thought about it, and the more I heard about what had happened, I realised that George couldn't be the murderer'. Maureen – unlike Laura and Margo – hadn't actually lived in Unitas Crescent with the Beatties as neighbours and so only knew George from her encounters with him at school. On the other hand, Laura and Margo had much more access to George and realised immediately that he wasn't capable of being the killer.

None of this indicates pluralistic ignorance, but rather the opposite: a pluralistic awareness. I wonder if the gendered nature of this pluralistic awareness served to constrain, rather than allow a challenge to the men who exercised power at the time. Even so, whether shared by men or women, it would appear that there had been no place for that pluralistic awareness to take root and then grow. Nor is there now any empirical way to judge how widespread that awareness might have been. However, for it to have become more widespread – and therefore much more dangerous to the flawed status quo – discussions about what had happened would have needed to have been heard in public places. This is not what Laura and Margo described: the discussions they remembered always seemed to take place in private and behind closed doors.

Taking all of this into consideration, it suggests that, at the time, people in the town might have been publicly silent about what had happened, rather than in denial. People could – and did – speak about Margaret's murder and their concerns about George's conviction; they were not silent. But these conversations took place in private settings; their voices were isolated and devoid of any wider platform that would have given them greater force. This public silence contributed to a lack of collective action.

The temptation here is to generalise and impose a neat and linear retrospective narrative onto what happened. I will resist that temptation. The past is always as messy, chaotic and incomplete as the present. Different individuals, perhaps at different times, have come to a similar understanding about what had taken place, rather than everyone reaching the same conclusion at the same time. They didn't speak all at once, but in fits and starts, and then eventually found their collective voice, although having done so there seems to have been a confusion as to what to do next; a confusion about how to act, as much as an unwillingness or reluctance to do so.

Of course I would like to think that it was a mature, moral decision that made me uneasy about George Beattie's conviction, but I cannot pretend that it was like this at all. If anything, I was stubborn and behaving like a teenager; I was refusing to accept what my so-called elders and betters were telling me. There was an uncompromising naivety in

my steadfast view that came with having few, if any, responsibilities. In some senses my support was for the principle of
justice, rather than for the individual himself. I'm not even all
that certain that I actually *liked* George Beattie and, thinking
back, I probably thought him as odd as everyone else did. I
certainly didn't think of him as a friend. Nor did I want to
take responsibility for the welfare of others, as I was far too
wrapped up in myself and my own youthful hopes and desires.

So what made me want to champion George Beattie's cause,
especially as that inevitably led to arguments with my father?
Looking back, I wonder if that was what I actually wanted.
Of course the attitudes and opinions of my sisters helped –
Alison was always keen to challenge people in authority and
the abandonment of her nursing career was a stark reminder
to me that beliefs should lead to action. Margaret's views
about George's conviction helped to shape mine and her certainty served to bolster my opinions.

But perhaps I am imposing an analysis that seems to now fit,
rather than describing one which is authentic. Looking back, I
think that my uncompromising naivety made me believe that
my fate was in my own hands; I was optimistic about what I
could do and who I could become. So if George Beattie was
innocent, we should say so and damn the consequences; the
truth should always conquer dishonesty and corruption. Facts
are more important than fiction; there really is such a thing
as 'truth'. I still think that.

And what about my sisters and their friends? Is this not
also about their optimism, about seeing their fate in their own
hands and believing that they could create a better society?
Theirs was a much braver optimism than my own, especially

as they stayed in Carluke. I again wonder to what extent their gender in the culture of 1970s Scotland inhibited what they discussed privately from becoming public. This is surely also where the personal becomes the political, or at least when it should do. However, politics did not seem to afford that individual and largely female optimism an organised outlet to mount a challenge to those men who had power, and who had used that power to convict George Beattie. So politics not only let George Beattie down, but also all those people in Carluke who knew in their hearts that he had been wrongly convicted.

Of course, and at the end of it all, this still leaves the elephant in the room.

If George Beattie did not kill Margaret McLaughlin, then who did?

But first, an opportunity presented itself to think a little more carefully about George's 'pseudo-confession'.

CHAPTER SIX

False and Pseudo-Confessions

'Memory is a complex thing'

I carried the drinks over from the counter and then settled on a comfortable sofa in the bar of the hotel where Beth and I were staying. She'd been on her feet all day, and was still suffering a little jet lag from her flight over from the USA to the conference in London where we were both speaking. So even though we had been friends for a number of years, I'd been a little reluctant to ask her for a favour. She had agreed, but on one condition – a glass of white wine.

Over the next few hours one glass became two and we eventually drained the bottle before I could finish my story about Margaret's murder and George's conviction, and then ask her opinion.

*

I imagine that the average person in the street simply doesn't understand why someone would admit to a crime that they hadn't committed, especially when such an admission will inevitably lead to arrest and prosecution, and, no doubt, also to spending a long time – sometimes a lifetime – in prison. At first glance, it just doesn't make any sense; it doesn't add up. And so, as the popular saying goes, people assume there's no smoke without fire.

Matters are further complicated by the fact that many of these 'false' confessions do usually contain accurate information about the crime. The person confessing can describe how the victim died; what weapon(s) was used; give a precise description of the crime scene; and perhaps a host of other details that makes the confession appear completely authentic and reliable.

It may be hard for people to imagine why anyone would do this, but a generation of research would now indicate that many do and that there are at least three different types of false confession: voluntary false confessions; coerced-compliant confessions; and, hardest of all to comprehend, coerced-internalised false confessions, when an innocent person actually comes to believe that they really *are* guilty of the crime, although they have no memory of actually committing it.

Innocent people might volunteer false confessions as the result of a desire for notoriety, the product of their underlying mental health issues, or to cover up for the real culprit. This type of false confession happens on a surprisingly regular basis, which is why police will often keep back certain details about how the crime was committed, so as to be better able to determine if the person 'confessing' is legitimate. These details are 'special knowledge' of the crime. After Muncie's trip in the aeroplane, and the publication of the details of the crime scene in a popular newspaper that was harder to do in Margaret's case.

The coerced-compliant false confession happens when the person being interviewed knows that they didn't actually commit the crime, but offers the confession in order to avoid the pressure and stress of being interviewed further. The person making this type of false confession is often submissive in the face of authority and so is easily manipulated and persuaded by the police to confess, wrongly believing that the truth will emerge later. They've reached a breaking point and so prioritise getting out of the interrogation and away from the clutches of the police. They are too emotional, scared and worn down to fully consider the consequences. It's a transient and fleeting response to the stresses that they are under, and once those stresses are removed, the 'confession' will be retracted.

Often the person making this type of false confession – in a sort of flawed cost/benefit analysis – reasons that it will all work out fine in the end, as it is obvious that they are innocent and, in the meantime, they can just 'confess', leave the station and get on with their lives.

It rarely works out that way, especially in the USA where detectives are trained to interview suspects in a particular manner called the Reid technique, which the recent Netflix series *Making a Murderer* has turned into a subject of popular debate.

John Reid was a former police officer in Chicago who would later become a polygraph expert. He believed that he could get even the most recalcitrant suspect to confess, and not through the common tactic of the time of beating a confession out of the suspect but through a technique that he had developed alongside and informed by his own self-taught understanding of human psychology.

Put very briefly, the Reid technique is accusatory rather than investigatory. Detectives confront a suspect with the details of the case and the evidence that they have against them at the start of their interviews. That evidence does not have to be genuine – American detectives are allowed to lie. They might state that they have found the suspect's fingerprints or DNA at the scene of the crime, or that witnesses have identified the suspect as being the culprit. None of this needs to be true, and often isn't. Detectives will also suggest more palatable reasons as to why the suspect committed the crime – even if they are in fact innocent. The suspect is offered excuses, such as 'we know that you didn't mean to do it', or 'you have put up with so much, it's no wonder that you just snapped'. This is called 'theme development' within the technique and can go on for many hours until the interviewee cracks and signs a confession, even if that confession is for a crime they did not commit.

*

The Reid technique was never formally adopted in Scotland, or indeed in England and Wales. In the United Kingdom, police officers are taught to use the PEACE model of interviewing and have been since the early 1990s. PEACE is a mnemonic and stands for Preparation and Planning; Engage and Explain; Account; Closure; and the final stage of the process, Evaluation. There are, however, a number of elements within the Reid technique that are useful to consider when thinking about why some people might have falsely confessed in the 1970s. After all, this was a period in Scotland before police interviews were routinely recorded and changes in legislation established how long a suspect could be interviewed for, as well as their right to have a solicitor present.

Let's bring these issues to life by considering the case of an American homicide detective who came to a startling insight about how he had been interviewing suspects, and how this might also provide clues about interviews in our own criminal justice system in the 1970s.

Jim Trainum was a Washington DC homicide detective who in 1994 realised that a suspect had confessed to a murder she clearly did not commit. As a result of her confession she had been charged with first degree murder, after which Trainum came across evidence that demonstrated her innocence. This started his interest in false confessions, and in 2016 he wrote *How the Police Generate False Confessions: An Inside Look at the Interrogation Room*. His book is essentially a plea for the US criminal justice system to adopt current British police interviewing techniques, but it is relevant here because we can see how some forms of interrogation lead to false confessions, without the Carluke police needing to have been using the Reid technique in the 1970s. In effect, Trainum offers a blueprint for how to go about extracting a false confession from a suspect.

Trainum warns against 'tunnel vision' within an investigation and emphasises the need for detectives to remain open minded. He notes that detectives who become 'locked in' to a suspect will ignore information that does not fit their case, and so they are no longer searching for the truth. He further states that the approach that most detectives take when interrogating a likely suspect has eight stages: to conclude the suspect is guilty; tell them there is no doubt of their guilt; block attempts by the suspect to deny guilt; suggest psychological or moral justifications as to why they committed the crime; lie about the strength of evidence against them; offer two explanations as to why they did it; get them to agree that they did commit the crime; and finally have them provide details about the crime.

Applying this blueprint to what we know happened to George during his police interviews is illuminating. We can see almost every stage being employed, albeit filtered through the lens of what was recorded by the police in their notebooks and what was later said by the prosecution. In other words, we have to make an imaginative leap into Carluke Police Station when George was being interviewed, as much as we have to interpret what was said, what was not said, and what was subsequently recorded, or not recorded, in a notebook or brought up at his trial.

It is obvious to me that the police believed that George was guilty, and he in turn did not help himself by continuing to offer information and suggesting scenarios that placed him at or at least near the scene of the murder. This, as discussed, was undoubtedly a feature of his underlying personality, that he was eager to please and would exaggerate to make himself appear more important. Only DC Semple seems to have been concerned that George was 'a bit simple', 'not really normal' and that he was adding to his statements 'for the sake of talking'. DC Semple does not, in other words, seem to believe what George was saying. Other police interviewers seemed more concerned with making a case against George than recognising that he was vulnerable, and that the stresses he was under – and how they went about interviewing him doubtless made him more prone to lie and exaggerate. They'd made up their minds that he must be guilty and decided that their job was to extract a confession from him; they had tunnel vision.

Did that mean that they adopted a confrontational and accusatory style in their interviewing? It is impossible to tell from what is recorded in the notebooks we have access to, but it isn't hard to believe that police officers would have been robust and uncompromising in how they treated their suspect. This is not to suggest that the detectives beat George, but is meant to imply that they were not going to let him out of the station until he had 'confessed'. They did not need to physically assault George as the psychological stress that he was under was enough to do the job for them. Of course, when he had confessed George would still not be let out of the station, or from the clutches of the criminal justice system, despite what he might have believed.

At this point in my thinking I looked again at the other features of Trainum's blueprint. We can see, or at the very least infer, most of the eight stages being gone through. George supposedly has 'special knowledge', and is therefore able to provide details about the crime. We are also offered a moral or psychological reason for that knowledge in that six men, two of whom were wearing tall hats, forced George to watch as Margaret was being murdered. No one really believed this to be true. We don't see two different explanations being offered as to why he had killed Margaret – motive was never really discussed – and, of course, George continued to deny his involvement in the murder itself. However, through what was recorded in the police notebooks, or was noted at his various appeals, all the other phases can be identified and they resulted in George being charged with murder.

Of course all of what I have described has to be set within the context of how the interview was conducted, as well as George's underlying personality. He'd been interviewed for several hours, by different police officers, late at night in the police station. He would have been tired, emotional and afraid. He would have felt that he would not have been allowed to leave that police station and go home until he gave the police what they wanted. Nor was there a lawyer present who might have been able to offer counsel. So George reached breaking point; he gave the police a pseudo-confession and then became so distressed that he had a mild epileptic fit, having to cling on to DC Johnston for support, sobbing uncontrollably.

One final issue is worth pursuing: the extraordinary details that George offers during these interrogations. There are the six men, two of whom were wearing tall hats with mirrors or glass in them; a small boy who waved to him from the train; George always 'going for a pee' behind a specific tree in the glen after leaving the house; and rabbits being skinned at a specific location 'for the pot'. Where do details such as this come from? How accurate might they be? Do they help us to assess guilt or innocence? These questions are best answered by considering what we know about memory and how memories are constructed, which brings us back to why I was having a glass of wine with Beth after our conference had ended.

*

In much the same way that I have suggested most people could never imagine themselves admitting to a crime that they didn't commit, it's also a good bet that they think of memory as simply a mechanism located in the brain that works like a form of recording device. In this common view people imagine that their memory records an experience and then, at a later date, they can play that memory back as a way of recalling the experience – almost as if you had a tape recorder in your head. Most people seem to believe that memory works in this straightforward, linear way: information enters through the ears and eyes and then somehow gets stored in the brain, to be brought out and re-played when you want to remember.

That's not how memory works.

Memory is a complex thing and the brain does not store a complete representation of events. Instead there is an intricate collection of events and these might not be stored as a coherent whole. In short, memory is often incomplete, fallible, subjective and malleable. Memories often change and can be transformed as a result of various processes. Indeed, Professor Elizabeth Loftus – the Beth I was sharing a bottle of wine with, and who also happens to be the world's leading memory expert – describes how memory is like a Wikipedia page, in that you can edit it and so can other people.

And we all know how unreliable Wikipedia can be.

There are three phases to the process that creates a memory: perception, storage and finally retrieval. Each of these phases is subjective and can be influenced by a variety of issues and events. This means that what is remembered is not necessarily objective and accurate, but is instead often partial and constructed.

At the perception stage, memories become distorted because people do not take in all the information that is available to them. Instead, they are selective; they are choosy about which pieces of information they become aware of and which they will ignore. An extreme example of this might be that a person with a gun to their head during a bank robbery will later remember everything about the gun, but know nothing at all about the person who was holding it. This is sometimes known as the 'weapon focus effect'.

After the information has been stored, this storage can become contaminated by the way in which that person is later questioned about the pieces of information that have become part of the memory. Asking leading questions that contain information which is suggestive but partial distorts and trans-forms a memory to the extent that, in extreme cases, it can supplant the actual memory entirely. A leading question about a car crash, for example, might be 'How fast were the cars going when they smashed into each other?' The verb 'smashed' suggests a particular speed, which the more neutral question 'How fast were the cars going when they hit each other?' does not. The person in the first example comes to believe that their stored memory of the accident was of two cars travelling too fast, when that might not have been the case at all.

What makes all of this even more problematic is that the person holding that 'memory' might be confident in how they express what they remember and provide an account which is often rich in detail. Yet confidence does not necessarily imply accuracy, at least as far as that memory is concerned. We should also be aware that the 'memory' can become contaminated if there has been a great deal of media coverage about the incident that is being remembered, and the individual who is being asked about the event has seen or read a great deal about that incident.

This is an important point to note in the Carluke case, and is why, for example, I have been keen to emphasise the importance of understanding Muncie's involvement with the *Daily Record* and how flying in their plane and then allowing photographs of the crime scene to be published during a live investigation was a mistake. Nor was it good practice for two detectives to walk a suspect through a crime scene. Though we don't know exactly what the three men discussed, is it too unreasonable to suggest that they discussed what had happened to Margaret, or where her possessions had been found? Are these not details that George could easily incorporate into his memory? There is a great deal of research that demonstrates this is very likely to have been exactly what happened.

Finally, at the retrieval stage, a number of factors can again contaminate the accuracy of the information which is being remembered. One such factor is the stress that a person might be under to remember the information. Someone experiencing a great deal of stress will have difficulty in recalling information about an event accurately. Repeatedly pressurising that person to come up with information about an event may lead to them filling in the gaps in their memory with contaminated information. No amount of probing will produce any accurate results if the information never entered their memory at all. You cannot truthfully remember something that you did not do, never saw or never actually witnessed.

Memory is therefore incomplete and partial, and can be shaped by the pressure that a person is under to remember. This in turn means that memories can be transformed by the way that an individual is questioned and the stress that they experience when trying to remember. Often what they produce will be rich in detail and expressed with confidence, but this does not necessarily mean that it is in any way accurate and can therefore be relied upon. Even so, and making it all even more problematic, the person offering these memories might sincerely believe them to be genuine.

How does all of this help us to make sense of the types of things that George said while being interrogated? We already know that he was eager to please and that he sought to avoid confrontation, but to what extent was the way that he was interviewed, and the pressure that he must have felt when he was being questioned in the police station, a contributory factor in what he said and about the information that he provided?

Let's consider again the rich detail that George provides in his interviews.

Some of these memories probably do recall events which had happened. George often used the shortcut to the station and so he is likely at some time in the past to have tripped in the glen; as a result he probably did cut his hand and have to wipe it on an handkerchief; and no doubt, with trainspotting as his hobby, there must have been an occasion when a small boy waved to him from one of the carriages. This memory also serves to suggest to the police that George is harmless, rather than dangerous. I don't mean to imply that George is using this memory in a consciously calculating way, but, under pressure, he is clearly retrieving and then presenting some memories in response to the questions that he is being asked. Perhaps he did once carry a case for Margaret, or maybe he simply wished that he had had the courage to offer to do so. What is less likely is that these events would all happen at the same time and on the night that Margaret was murdered. Rather, George is conflating discrete memories of actual events into a distinct memory of a specific event. The detail that he offers is therefore rich, which gives his account of the night in question the appearance of authenticity.

Other information that George provides seems to be the result of contamination. For example, blood is mentioned. George (and nearly everyone else in the town) would have been aware that Margaret had been repeatedly stabbed as this was widely reported and being discussed locally. He remembers gutting rabbits and the blood that produces, which, in turn, became a false memory about Margaret's blood. He had already said something similar to a work colleague. His knowledge that the knife that had been found – and which was believed to have been the murder weapon – is the reason that George describes using a much smaller 'linoleum' knife to gut the rabbits. He probably did gut a rabbit, or at least had been present when this had happened for, by all accounts, some of his brothers liked hunting. In fact, this smaller 'linoleum' knife that he describes is perhaps one of the most revealing exchanges as it shows us the extent of the contamination within his interviews. We have to infer that George is emphasising its size specifically because he has become aware through what the police have told him of the much larger knife that they wrongly believed had killed Margaret.

George himself seems to have been aware that some of the information which he was offering was nonsense. We see this most vividly in his comments about not being able to urinate. Undoubtedly he must have urinated on a number of times in the glen, but not on every occasion when he walked there. He is merely trying to appease his police interrogators by providing information in response to their questions. He wants to cooperate as he has nothing to hide; he is eager to make his interrogators happy; he likes to be liked, and so he wants to help. As a consequence, he answers their questions. However, in the absence of a genuine memory of the events that took place that night, he stitches together bits and pieces of other memories, along with the contaminated information that the police have provided, until they become his whole narrative.

The most damaging information that George provided related to the six men, two of whom, he claimed, had worn tall hats with mirrors, or glass in them. As I have indicated, this was an allusion to the pop group Slade and his memory of watching them on *Top of the Pops*. Slade were perhaps the most popular band of the early 1970s, with six number-one hits and a total of sixteen singles in the UK top ten. In June/ July 1973 they reached number one with their single 'Skweeze Me, Pleeze Me' and had appeared on *Top of the Pops* with two of the four-piece band wearing hats similar to those described by George. If this was a memory of them that he was recreating, why did George state that six men were involved?

It does not seem coincidental to me that George was one of six brothers. This is not intended to imply that he or his brothers were involved in the murder, but is simply a reflection that when he was under pressure and in the stress of the interview George settled on a familiar number.

George would later claim that the information about being forced to watch Margaret's death by this strange group of men had been fed to him by the police who were interviewing him. I have no way of verifying this claim. But if it is true we can see in it a form of 'theme development' from the Reid technique. The suggestion offers a way of making George feel more comfortable about explaining why he might have been present when Margaret was murdered. He accepts their offer but still maintains his innocence; he is trying to give the police what they are seeking, while at the same time continuing to deny any involvement with having murdered Margaret.

'I canny say no more. I didn't do it. It was they six.'

*

Beth Loftus had never heard of George Beattie or Margaret McLaughlin, and so over our bottle of wine I outlined the story to her and explained everything that George had said in his various police interviews. I also described how George's statements had become more developed and embellished as time went on, and outlined for her something of George's educational and psychological background. Beth asked a few questions and sought some clarification on a number of points, but listened carefully to what I had to say. Eventually I finished my outline and then, peering at me through her Dita spectacles, Beth smiled and said, 'He's just merged bits and pieces of experience from different places – it's what people do when they construct false memories. What he said is false. It's not true.'

She didn't need to be told anything else; for the world's foremost expert in memory, it was that straightforward.

In George's 'pseudo-confession', what we glimpse is not the truth of Margaret's murder and George's role – or rather non-role – within it. All he has ever said about the attack on Margaret is this pseudo-confession, and what we see in it is the product of his confused desire to please the police; memories

131

which had become contaminated by information which was already in the public domain, or which he had gained access to from his police trips to the glen, or which had been fed to him; and his stitching together of different memories from multiple events into one specific, extraordinary whole and which was then readily inferred as constituting guilt.

This might seem like being wise after the event, but I do still wonder to what extent the police themselves really believed what George had told them. DC Semple clearly did not. Was he the only sceptical police officer, or were there more? Early on in my research I interviewed George's original solicitor, who has now long since retired. He stated that George's arrest was 'the talk of the police', and as my research progressed several former detectives came forward to share, off the record, their concerns about the investigation. This would suggest that DC Semple was not the only officer who was unconvinced about what George was saying. Yet what is rarely considered in the study of 'false confessions' is why the police come to believe, or in this case come to accept, what they are being told, when it is often obvious that what is being described by a suspect is inaccurate; is the product of information contamination; or is simply caused by the stress that the interviewee is under.

Do the police go along with the false confession because they believe it to be genuine, or are there perhaps instrumental, institutional pressures to get a suspect – no matter whether innocent or guilty – charged with the offence? Are there sometimes pressures to 'fit up' someone who is believed to be guilty, even if there is little or no evidence to prove the case? Is that morally wrong, or can it be justified on the utilitarian grounds that an offender has been removed from the community and therefore cannot harm anyone else? This is often described as 'noble cause corruption', as the rule-bending – the 'fitting up' – is a means of securing a conviction that might not otherwise have occurred. Does that thought reassure you, or make you feel profoundly uncomfortable?

Even if an individual police officer comes to believe that a confession is false, how easy would it be to convince others that this was the case, especially if those officers were more senior and therefore exercised greater power? In this situation, does the officer simply turn a blind eye to what he or she knows to be true and get on with their job? What if several are having to turn a blind eye? This would surely become much more of a collective denial of the truth, perhaps based on working cultures of who gets promoted and who does not, loyalty and secrecy in the face of adversity and the codes of silence that this would generate.

These questions don't just apply to the police, but can be widened more generally to include the public and the broader culture in which we all live. Frankly, it is easy to criticise the police, but don't we deserve criticism too?

Why do we accept a version of events that we know to be incorrect? Why do we remain silent, and so collude, rather than challenge what we know to be an injustice? Don't we also turn a blind eye to those things that we know but would prefer not to know? Don't we often walk on by, refusing to acknowledge what we have just witnessed? We have all at some time in our lives and for various reasons 'looked the other way', 'worn blinkers', 'lived a lie', and as a result have been able to go on with our lives in 'wilful ignorance'.

Of course, the alternative is to intervene and take personal responsibility to rectify what has happened, or to challenge authority and demand that the injustice is put right. How common is that? What sort of people challenge others in this way, especially those who are in positions of authority, and in what circumstances does that challenge get mounted?

I might not have been able to mount my challenge in the past, but perhaps I could do so in the present. It was time to go back to Carluke again.

CHAPTER SEVEN

A Criminological Autopsy in Carluke

An intimate space for a murder

How can we make sense of both the specific circumstances and wider context in which one person kills another?

For some years I have used an approach which I have called a 'criminological autopsy' to try to answer this question. It's a combination of a number of different approaches and research methods, including a widely used procedure known as a 'psychological autopsy'. This was developed in the 1970s by an American clinical psychologist called Edwin Schneidman to reconstruct the life of a person who has committed suicide through analysing their letters or other writings that they might have left behind; talking with people who saw them in the days leading up to their death; and discussing with them how that person might have been behaving. In this way inferences can be drawn about the deceased person's thoughts, feelings and emotions. The goal is to ascertain what might have motivated them to take their own life.

My criminological autopsy does something similar, but with the obvious difference that I am trying to reconstruct the life of a person who was murdered and, by doing so, attempting to deduce who might have committed that murder. This means that I am often trying to think about two people – the person who was murdered and the person who killed them. However, as with the psychological autopsy, I am keen to talk with the family or friends of the person who was murdered, so as to build up a picture of their life, as well as reading any documents that might have been left behind or which may be relevant to the crime. Sometimes I will engage the help of a local journalist, or a retired detective who had worked on the case to share with me what they know.

Finally, I also walk in the spaces where the dead person once lived and worked, and, if the place where they were killed is known, I will visit that site too.

It is surprising how much practical and emotional insight you can gain from simply visiting the place in which a murder has occurred. There are some obvious questions to ask:

- Was the space overlooked or isolated?
- Was it necessary to have a car to drive there, or could you get to the site on foot?
- Was the crime scene well lit, or in an area that was dark and desolate?
- Who would normally use this space and at what times?

136

- Is it normally busy and populated, or isolated and deserted?
- Was there any CCTV coverage that might offer clues as to the identity of the killer?
- Could the killer have taken a different route away from the site after the murder had been completed, or would he have had to retrace his steps?

Thinking about all of these questions affords a great deal of information about who the likely perpetrator might have been, where he might live or work, and even what sort of work he might do.

Nor do I shy away from thinking about what might have motivated the murderer, even if motivation is rarely discussed within criminology. It is not always helpful to discuss motivation within a police investigation, even if this is often the very first question in crime dramas, as that might not necessarily push the investigation forwards. A killer's motivations could be common to many people and therefore unhelpful in identifying a suspect; alternatively, the motivation could be so bizarre and idiosyncratic as to be meaningless. As a consequence, our police are taught to be much more focused on access and opportunity – they will consider who had access to the victim before he or she died, and how that access could have been used to kill. Some killers might have access to the victim but no opportunity to use that access to murder their target, while others might have lots of opportunities but no access at all. And, in all likelihood – in reality, if rarely in crime fiction – the killer and the victim have usually been in some form of relationship.

All of this raises the question: who would have had access to Margaret on the night that she was murdered, and who would also have had the opportunity to use that access to kill her?

At this point in any investigation I turn to ethnography. Ethnography involves the researcher spending significant periods of time within the culture that is being studied: listening to conversations; interviewing key participants; gathering documents; and observing the behaviour of people within that culture as they go about their daily lives. It often involves a long-term and many-sided relationship with the people involved in the event. Academics within the social sciences will usually describe how they gained access to these people or the organisations that they want to research and whether or not their role as a researcher should be 'overt' – open and publicly acknowledged – or 'covert', where the researcher disguises what he is doing and what his true interests might be. There are further questions related to whether the researcher is an active member of the group, or is simply observing what is happening.

Given my personal history with Carluke and the fact that until recently all three of my sisters lived in the town, I am already closer, more immersed in the community, than I usually would be when undertaking a criminological autopsy. I did not want to be clandestine about my intentions in looking into Margaret's murder, or hide what I thought about the case when I was a teenager or now. Indeed, I used the opportunity of speaking at the town library to publicly announce what I was currently researching and then handed out my business cards to anyone in the audience who might like to contact me to talk about the case.

I have used the technique of criminological autopsy for a number of years, in different research situations and in a variety of countries. I drove the eight miles from Thomas Hamilton's house in Stirling to Dunblane, trying to imagine what he might have been thinking about on the twenty-minute journey to the primary school where, on 13 March 1996, he took the lives of sixteen children and their teacher, and where he then killed himself; I walked Dunblane's streets and drank in its pubs; I spoke with the very few people who were prepared to talk to me; I visited the memorial to the children and their teacher; and read and re-read the public inquiry that investigated the country's worst ever mass murder.

I used the same technique in Whitehaven in Cumbria to make sense of Derrick Bird's spree shootings, when in June 2010 he killed twelve people and injured eleven others, before taking his own life. I hired a taxi from the rank where he had once worked and was driven by one of his former colleagues on the circuitous route he took in the countryside surrounding Whitehaven. I stayed in the town and struck up conversations with people who knew Bird, or who had heard about the case; I drank in several pubs and had my meals in local restaurants – always making clear that I was a criminologist engaged in research.

This immersion is vital to my investigations. If I am searching for the truth about a murder – even one committed nearly fifty years ago – and hope to come to conclusions that will be accepted more broadly, I need to explain fully how I have gone about my research, and have arrived at my conclusions. This is the equivalent of my old maths teacher saying 'I want to see your workings-out'. So I want to walk and then describe for you the route that Margaret would have taken, looking at all the houses that she would have passed as she made her way to the station. Who might she have seen, and who might have spotted her? How long would this walk have taken if she had arrived and caught the train? Of course she tragically never managed to get to the station, but how far was it from her home to the place where she was attacked? The attack lasted only a few moments, but why were there no witnesses? I wondered if perhaps there was a blind spot on the route that had been exploited by her killer.

These questions could only be answered by walking the route through Carluke and by retracing Margaret's fateful footsteps.

There is an echo here with what is sometimes called 'psycho-geography'. In other words, when psychology and geography are combined so that we can try to understand the environment's impact on an individual's behaviour and emotion. Walking slowly through the landscape is central to psycho-geography, all the time trying to see and take note of things that might have been overlooked, or ignored by those who hurry through the space without really seeing. My goal is to try to make sense of a space – specifically, a space where there has been a murder.

*

When I had reached the stage of my research that involved me re-investigating the murder, my first priority was to get back to Carluke and walk in Colonel's Glen and in and around the streets that formed the shortcut to the station. I was accompanied on my walk by my brother-in-law, Willie, who is married to my sister Margaret. Willie is a former paramedic, and in the course of his work he had got to know the people of this area well. He had often attended patients in both streets. He thought of Glenburn Terrace and Unitas Crescent as 'full of decent, working-class people', a characterisation that chimed with what Margo and Laura remembered from growing up there.

Willie seemed to know everyone: on our walk from the High Street to the glen, he had to stop every few yards to exchange greetings. As he walked away he'd invariably say to me, 'Do you remember him?' and I would usually have to reply in the negative. Willie would then fill me in with information about the person he had been speaking to, and how they would have known my parents, or my sisters. I quickly realised that Willie was taking on the role that a local journalist or a detective played when I undertook a criminological autopsy. He was using his local knowledge and connections to allow me to experience the place that I was researching from a truly indigenous perspective, and which I might not have seen had I been by myself. These conversations rarely held any criminological value – they were about events in the news, or snippets of information about mutual acquaintances – but they made me feel slightly conflicted. They reinforced a sense that I have always had about both being connected to but at the same time distanced from Carluke. It was Willie who knew these people, not me, even if he had not actually been brought up in the town. Carluke had once been my home, but now I had to accept that I really was an outsider – I am both connected to, but distanced from these people at the same time.

At the top of the High Street we turned left at the traffic lights and walked down Kirkton Street. Within a few hundred yards we passed the site of the the old post office, which had been knocked down to make way for new flats. A few yards further on, we came to the solicitors Forrest, Campbell & Anderson, and as I used to go to school with Douglas Forrest I felt that I should stop by and say hello. Douglas was with a client and so I couldn't actually see him. Later I wondered if I had only done this to remind myself – and, unconsciously, Willie too – that I had indeed once lived in Carluke, even if I hadn't actually seen Douglas in at least twenty years.

We walked on, and passed Station Road. I thought that perhaps we should turn down there to get to the station, and made to do so. 'No – you keep walking down here,' replied Willie, gesturing straight ahead, and it was then that I realised that I had never actually been in Glenburn Terrace or Unitas Crescent before. Such are the divisions that even a small town can hide. I might have regularly caught the train in my youth, but I'd never used the shortcut Margaret had taken in 1973, and so I had never walked through Unitas Crescent or Glenburn Terrace. This day, over forty-five years later, was to be the first time I had walked these streets – and again I felt conflicted. As a child I had known just one tiny part of what life in Carluke had been like, and how it had been experienced by the majority of the people who were living there.

But, if I am honest, I was also pleased by this geographic ignorance, as I could come to those streets with a genuinely fresh pair of eyes. What I might see had the potential to make me think very differently about what I had read.

We kept on walking, past the old bus station, which is now a supermarket, and then turned right beside what used to be Loch Park Stadium, where Carluke Rovers played. I remembered that there was a running track around the edges of the football pitch, and this would have been where Margo came second in her race at the Highland games. Inevitably, it has all been redeveloped and upmarket houses now stand on the site. I wondered what had happened to Carluke Rovers.

In the near distance I spotted a train whistling past. It was clearly an intercity making its way to Glasgow Central and, based on its colours, looked like one of the Virgin West Coast fleet. Undoubtedly it had travelled up that morning from Euston, although it wouldn't stop at Carluke. Carluke station is for local trains from Lanark which are heading for Wishaw, Motherwell and then on to Glasgow Central; it is too provincial to be a stop for intercity trains from Euston.

I quickly located number 30 Glenburn Terrace, where Margaret had once lived, and noticed how close the house is to Unitas Crescent and the railway tracks beyond. I told Willie that I wanted to knock on the door and, for the first time, he looked a little surprised. He had been guiding me and now, almost imperceptibly, I was taking charge. Knocking unannounced on people's doors – doorstepping – is an inevitable part of my criminological world, especially when trying to uncover the truth from people who would prefer to keep it concealed.

'I'm just curious about what the owners might know about the murder,' I explained to Willie, trying to reassure him that this was all normal practice.

I walked up a small path to the front door and, as I did so, I noticed a stone that had been hand-painted with '30, Nut House'.

I knocked on the door, but no one was at home.

Willie looked relieved.

'OK,' I said, 'let's walk Unitas Crescent.'

From this end of Glenburn Terrace you turn right and then after about twenty yards enter Unitas Crescent. The houses are in the high even numbers, starting at 108. The junction with Glenburn Terrace is approximately opposite number 100 Unitas Crescent. As we walked down the street a few people started to take notice of us, standing out as strangers on a quiet residential street, although no one actually spoke to us. Quite quickly we came to the gap in the houses that forms the shortcut Margaret would have walked through on her way to the railway station. I discovered then that this gap is between numbers 78 and 76 Unitas Crescent. I walked into the gap but then turned around again as I wanted to go and see number 48, where the Beatties had once lived. This was some way further down the street, away from the cut-through. Once again our presence was drawing attention and so I started to say 'Good morning' to see if I could initiate a conversation. Still no one spoke to either Willie or me, but many nodded by way of acknowledging my greeting.

'OK, Willie, let's do some timings,' I said, and we retraced our steps back to 30 Glenburn Terrace. 'Margaret came out of the house just after ten to eight to catch the three minutes past eight to Glasgow. Let's see how long the walk would have taken her.'

Setting the stopwatch on my phone, I took a deep breath and stood quietly for a few seconds before starting off on the route that Margaret would have taken on the night that she was murdered. I used those seconds to remember that this would have been the last time that she would have closed her front door and called 'Goodbye' over her shoulder to her parents as she pulled it shut; the last time that she would walk in the streets where she had been raised and had played as a child. She was only minutes away from her death. I exhaled and, with Willie following, walked the route, my eyes darting here and there so as to soak up everything that I could see.

It took us one minute and twenty seconds to get from 30 Glenburn Terrace to the gap in Unitas Crescent. That seemed very quick. I wondered if perhaps we had walked too fast and so we went back to number 30 and did the walk again, deliberately walking more slowly. Still not satisfied, a third time as well. The timings were all very similar. It took about one minute, twenty seconds to get from her home to the gap between 78 and 76 Unitas Crescent, which opened into the shortcut to the station.

After checking the timing for the third time, we continued through the gap and walked into the open area that led towards the station. Once again I timed this part of the journey several times, although I was well aware that Margaret had actually never made it to the station. The average time that it took us was one minute, ten seconds. All of this is to say that if Margaret had not been attacked, the journey from her home to the station would have been made in under three minutes, five minutes at most if she had been walking especially slowly.

She would have been in plenty of time to buy a ticket and catch the train into Glasgow.

I thought about how her life and those of her family would have been so very different if she had completed that journey.

Willie and I walked on and entered the station, then retraced our steps back to the gap, peering into Colonel's

Glen as we did so. There was no footpath to take us down to the bottom of the glen and so we stayed at the top, surveying the rubbish that had been left by successive generations of locals. We walked on, and then I stood for a few minutes in the space immediately after the shortcut where Margo and Laura had once played and where Margaret had been attacked before being dragged into Colonel's Glen. I looked around me, trying to make sense of what had happened. It seemed like an intimate space for a murder to have taken place – made all the more so by the fact that it was overlooked by some of the houses on Unitas Crescent. This was a surprise. I was expecting to find a blind spot that the killer had exploited; the fact that there wasn't one made me think again about Margaret's attacker. There might not have been CCTV footage – which we now have in most murder investigations – but there could have been the original form of CCTV: scores of human eyes, scrutinising eyes, watching and observing the attack unfold.

It was a murder that had to have been completed within a very few minutes, certainly before anyone got off the train that Margaret had intended to catch – the 8.03 to Glasgow, or indeed before anyone else decided to use the same shortcut to catch the next train leaving Carluke. It had to be over before someone in Unitas Crescent went into their kitchen to switch on the kettle to make a cup of tea and happened to glance out of their window.

Then, once Margaret was dead, the murderer needed to get away undetected – no small feat given that he'd have been elated, excited, or perhaps even scared; he would have been emotionally 'high'.

Most certainly he would have also have been covered in

Margaret's blood, but there were no witnesses to anyone walking about with blood on their clothes, or acting strangely or even out of the ordinary. I remembered Muncie's statement to the newspapers that the killer would have 'signs of murder on his person'. Muncie had got that right, and my growing understanding of what had happened started to wrap itself around me like a dark cloak, as I stood there imagining the crime scene and understanding what risks Margaret's killer had taken that night.

That's the problem with knowing too much about murder. It sometimes seeps into my consciousness and my soul. The violent and the irrational start to make sense to me; I can begin to differentiate between the murders that are poorly planned and executed, and those which have a degree of professionalism. This murder seemed poorly planned, even if it was successful, because of all the risks that the killer had taken.

Risks?

Margaret's killer didn't have much time to play with; he knew that he had to act quickly, to kill her and then disappear if he didn't want to be caught. He knew that the walk to the station wouldn't have taken Margaret more than a few minutes, and that at the station it was likely that there would have been people to protect her. He had to attack her with speed and, crucially, without being seen either before, during or after the attack. Her murder was a gamble – or a calculated risk at the very least.

But this murderer was lucky, and luck was undoubtedly a factor in his choosing to kill Margaret on that night, at that time and in that specific location.

He knew that he could kill Margaret at that time without

being seen and then disappear just as successfully. I am almost certain he knew that because he had watched her walk down Unitas Crescent and realised that there were no children playing in the gap beside Colonel's Glen. Margo wasn't there, but was instead resting after running lap after lap in preparation for the Highland games, and neither were any of her friends on the swings or the roundabout. They'd probably gone indoors to seek shelter from the wind and the rain. He was also lucky that Margaret was by herself, because that made him feel more confident. The killer realised that this was his chance; perhaps a chance he had been hoping would come his way for some time. I don't believe that Margaret's killer 'snapped', instead I'm certain that he had watched and waited and planned; he could be controlled when he needed to be. As I had thought when I first reconsidered the case – based on what had been written in the newspapers at the time – he was both organised and disorganised, and so I would expect to find aspects of both of these traits in his non-offending life.

At last I understood how he could have killed Margaret and, just as importantly, how he could have avoided being seen with 'signs of murder on his person'. He had to be quick, but speed itself was just a small part in the murder and how he avoided being apprehended on the night, and during the subsequent investigation. Everything that happened that night was about geography and the specific layout of the streets, the location of the shortcut to the station, sight lines and how this allowed Margaret's killer to be able to enter and leave the glen without being seen. In other words, this was all about where he lived. Everything that followed was about Muncie's confirmation bias that George Beattie was guilty, and his refusal to consider other, and more likely suspects. That was lucky for the real killer too. I can now only speculate, but I wonder if Muncie – Scotland's 'top detective' – had actually followed a similar line of reasoning to my own but made the evidence fit Beattie, rather than keeping an open mind to the possibility of another culprit. The forensic report about the knife must have come as a shock to him, but by then he had too much to lose. He couldn't admit that his psychic powers had failed him; he had to make the charge stick on Beattie.

I closed my eyes, attempting to erase the pictures that were forming in my mind of Margaret's killer scuttling away with a bloody knife in his hand. The sense that I'd just had of truly understanding what had happened was now replaced by a creeping depression and my total lack of surprise – nothing here was mysterious, or remarkable. If the police had done their jobs at the time, they would have caught the real culprit. That thought made me miserable; it could all have been so different. As I stood there, blinking and looking around to take in the crime scene and its relation to the houses in Unitas Crescent, I came to another degree of understanding, and found that I began to make an estimation of where I believe that the killer would have lived, according to my emerging hypothesis.

This is what I believe happened.

The killer was watching Margaret from his window as she walked down the street carrying her bag and case. It was obvious that she was going to the station. He let her walk into the shortcut while, almost simultaneously, he left his house by the back door and walked through his back garden carrying a knife that he had picked up in the kitchen. His back garden bordered the shortcut and, if I am right, he would have reached Margaret just as she emerged onto the path and made her way further into the glen. He'd come up behind her, overpowered and killed her, then retraced his steps just as quickly and returned to his house via the back door, carrying the murder weapon.

It would all have been over in just a few short minutes.

Margaret's body wouldn't have been cold by the time he had returned home. He would still have been drenched in the blood spatter from the multiple knife wounds he had inflicted. It would have been on his clothes and on his hands and face; it would have seeped into his hair. There would have been marks on his body too, if Margaret had been able to fight back which, even if this isn't noted in any documentation that I have seen, is more than likely. Even so, he'd have achieved his murderous objective and, now safely inside, he could dispose of all his bloody clothes, wash away all the incriminating evidence and, as best as he could, try to compose himself before anyone found out what had happened.

But then, of course, he had to avoid being apprehended once Margaret's body had been found and the police started their house-to-house enquiries. If my hypothesis was right, he *must* have been interviewed in the days after the murder and I started to wonder what he had said to deflect the police's attention. Could he really have regained control so quickly after the murder?

I kicked a small stone and watched it bounce along the ground until it came to rest. This distraction broke the spell and allowed me to think about something other than the murder.

I didn't tell any of this to Willie, and instead we turned in the direction of Glenburn Terrace and Unitas Crescent.

*

On this return into Unitas Crescent people started to make eye contact and one or two responded to my greetings. Perhaps they had got used to our presence. I didn't try to ask any questions and nor did I answer those that were put to us as to why we were on the street. It went a little against the totally overt stance of my research, but my head was still buzzing with the ideas that had started to form in my mind.

Willie and I made our way back to 30 Glenburn Terrace and I noticed that a middle-aged man – obviously the owner – was walking purposefully towards the front door with his dog.

This was our chance.

'Hello,' I said, and introduced myself as a criminologist interested in the area. The man was understandably a bit wary but nonetheless we spent a few minutes exchanging pleasantries. I asked him how long he had been living in the house and he said he'd been there for twenty years, but had lived in another part of Carluke before then. He asked me what I was doing and at that point I felt it only fair to explain my links to Carluke, and the fact that I was looking into what had happened in 1973.

'You mean the murder?' he asked.

'Yes,' I replied.

'The Beattie murder?'

'Yes – what do you think about that?' I queried.

'You'd have to ask around, but he seems innocent to me.'

He then excused himself, explaining that he was on the backshift and so needed to get ready for work.

I was intrigued by this reference to 'the Beattie murder'. It was Margaret who was murdered and George that was convicted of her murder, but this man had conflated these details. I wondered how many other people in Carluke did the same, erasing poor Margaret and confusing George's circumstances with hers. Their very different tragedies had become so completely entwined over time that Margaret had disappeared from view. I wondered to what extent the living supersede the dead in our imaginations, or if this was a specifically criminological phenomenon. Do people remember the victim, or the perpetrator? Is it Ian Huntley or Holly Wells and Jessica Chapman that we recall when we think back to the events that took place in Soham in 2002? Is it Dale Cregan, rather than Fiona Bone and Nicola Hughes, that we first think of when remembering the murders that he committed in 2012?

Willie and I kept walking and I took the opportunity to ask him if he'd object to us taking a detour to the police station where George had been interviewed. He readily agreed. I had started to think about the police investigation again, and couldn't think of a better place to channel my thoughts.

It didn't take us more than ten minutes to walk from Unitas Crescent to Carluke Police Station, although a lot has changed since 1973. The station is now closed to the public and anyone in need of help is directed by a notice on the door to Lanark Police Station. Even so, there was a police car in the drive and – as with 30 Glenburn Terrace – I knocked on the door. No one answered and so we began to walk away, but at that moment a young blond man emerged from the back of the station and somewhat suspiciously asked 'Can I help you?'

Once again I introduced myself. The officer told me his

name and it turned out that he was about to start his shift. The station might seemingly be closed to the public, but that didn't mean that there weren't officers who worked in the building.

'I know you,' he said, looking slightly unable to place where he knew me from.

Once I'd mentioned my criminology work in the media, he told me his girlfriend, who works in CID, loves true crime documentaries, and so everything became clearer. It also provided me with an opening to chat for a few minutes longer. It transpired that, despite being so fresh-faced, he'd been a police officer for ten years, though he was thinking of giving it all up and becoming a train driver.

'Do you know you can earn sixty thousand pounds a year driving a train?' he asked me.

I shook my head, amazed at this salary, which was clearly in excess of what a police officer earns. I then asked the police officer if he knew about the murder that had taken place in 1973. He didn't, though he had recently moved to Carluke to look after some relatives who lived in Unitas Crescent. Small towns must produce coincidences like this all the time, but they never cease to amaze me.

We discussed the police officer's career ambitions a little further and then, as I was about to go, and perhaps just to be friendly, he asked quite casually, 'Did you know that this part of the station used to be a mortuary?'

Neither Willie nor I were aware of this, but it is the sort of detail that helps to give me an impression of a place and it also prompted a question. Could it have been possible that George had been interviewed just a few yards away from where Margaret's body had been laid?

We took our leave of the constable and I asked Willie if he had ever had to visit the police station to recover a dead body. Willie had a vague recollection of this having happened but he couldn't be certain.

We were trying to make sense of events that took place in Carluke in 1973, but in under fifty years the police station had been closed to the public, the post office and bus station had disappeared, and the spaces that had once been for everyone's use had been gobbled up by housing developments. We therefore have to rely on the memories of the living to reconnect us to the past – even the recent past. This especially seems to be the case if these places, or the people who once occupied them, are not 'the great and the good'. Those with more official standing in the community are better able to either resist, or to prompt these changes that I have described, rather than simply becoming passive recipients. The great and the good are also more practised at writing things down and getting their thoughts published in the newspapers, or collected in the books that fill the library's shelves. This becomes the 'history' to be celebrated in Carluke's Market Square.

Everything else gets forgotten. The police officer that I had spoken to had never heard of the murder of Margaret McLaughlin, even though he had relatives living in Unitas Crescent.

Institutions, as much as people, are unable to resist change. I've mentioned the bus depot and the post office, but what about British Rail (it had been a Virgin Train that I had seen whistling past Glenburn Terrace), or even the old asylums? These institutions are often sold into private hands and converted into profit-making enterprises, or perhaps just expensive flats. The local football stadium and tennis club had become private housing within one generation. Those old, shared, democratic spaces that people used to occupy in Carluke, these institutions that were once so heavily relied on, are but collateral damage in the face of neoliberalism's ever impatient, private expansionism. What happened in Carluke is simply a microcosm of what happens in towns all over the UK; a creeping dismantling of community and those who once served it. In its wake Willie and I were left trying to make sense of the cultural world we once inhabited and which, in turn, had made us who we are. Soon, when we no longer have a personal memory that we can share and when the few remaining 'state' institutions have all disappeared, or been privatised, who will remember then? Will there still be solidarity among people, or just individuals thinking about themselves?

Even the young police officer had wanted to give up the public service of policing to pursue an income that he felt better suited his place in this neoliberal world. Who can blame him?

As this was all flooding through my consciousness, a melancholy descended once more – this time because I know that we cannot privatise community. 'Love thy neighbour' cannot be leveraged for profit. I also knew that these feelings were for another day; this wasn't why I was in Carluke. I needed to turn my mind back to the matter at hand.

I suggested to Willie that we walk back down the High Street towards Rankin Gait and get a cup of tea. I wanted to gather my thoughts and perhaps channel Carluke's most famous son, to see where he might lead me. I don't know if he would have thought it was appropriate, but I wanted to analyse and process everything I'd seen on our walk from Glenburn Terrace, through Unitas Crescent and into the shortcut to the station where Margaret had been murdered.

I wanted to apply some rigour to my thinking.

*

My wife Anne joined us as we reached Rankin Gait, and I left her and Willie drinking their tea, while I excused myself to go outside to write up my notes. I sat at a table with a view of the intersection of the High Street with Chapel Street and Hamilton Street. I was less than a hundred feet away from the toy shop where my parents had treated me on Saturdays, though it had long since disappeared. And then the past seemed to become the present. Some young boys slipped into view, although I quickly realised that they were all smoking, rather than wanting to buy toys or play tennis. They cupped their cigarettes in their hands so as to hide them from direct view, seemingly unaware that it was perfectly obvious what they were doing when they blew smoke into the air around them. I don't think Dr Rankin would have approved.

I plunged back into my notes, quickly realising that certain words and phrases kept appearing in what I had managed to scribble down on our walk. 'Intimate', 'he'd have to be quick', 'seems like a risk', 'all over in seconds', 'lucky' and 'local' kept cropping up. This last word in particular occurred on numerous occasions. Was I meaning Carluke, or where the murder had occurred? The murder site – that liminal space – would probably only have been known to the people who lived in the streets adjoining Unitas Crescent: this was long before Google Maps could direct you down a convenient side street. But I realised that there was more to it. Margaret's killer had to be local to those streets because living in that area gave him the opportunity to observe and keep watch; it gave him a chance to listen and to know; and, perhaps through that knowledge, to feel bitter and angry.

I thought back to my original profile and how I had suggested that Margaret's killer had acted to save face.

I wondered if perhaps he had seen Margaret's sister walk the same route when she had gone to the station to catch her earlier train. Was this what had prompted his anger to rise and then boil over? Was he sitting alone, slowly getting angrier, playing over and over and over in his head perceived slights from the past that he felt that Margaret had inflicted upon him? Perhaps not sitting, that didn't feel right, but pacing up and down and letting his anger keep time with his footsteps. His pacing would become more insistent, until he felt that he had to act; it was like an obsession. Murder always has a context and, in my experience, it is never the result of a sudden rush of passion.

Over and over and over in his head; repetitious – just like the wounds that he'd inflict one after another on Margaret's body.

Re-reading my notes I realised that 'local' was still too broad a description. If I was right, I could be much more specific.

Margaret's killer lived in Unitas Crescent, in one of the even-numbered houses that started at 108 and went down to the gap between numbers 78 and 76. Below number 74 was too far away to have been able to observe if there were children playing outside near the glen and to have seen Margaret on her walk to the station – unless he was in the street by that stage. That seemed unlikely, although I had considered this a possibility. What if he had spotted Margaret as he was walking home from work, either from the train or the bus station, or perhaps he saw her having walked up Unitas Crescent towards the gap (as George Beattie would later claim that he had done)? What if he carried a knife with him, perhaps as part of his job, as a butcher or a carpenter? It was around eight in the evening, but perhaps he was late getting home from work, or had stopped off to have a drink with colleagues.

Rather than having observed Margaret, what if he had encountered her by chance?

I was faced with two competing hypotheses, and in such instances I tend to apply the principle of Occam's razor.

William of Occam, a Franciscan friar, was credited with saying that 'entities are not to be multiplied without necessity'. In other words, you should 'shave' away unnecessary assumptions and cut apart two similar conclusions – just like a razor. Occam's razor suggests that simpler solutions are more likely to be correct than those which are complex. So when presented with opposing hypotheses to solve a problem, Occam's razor recommends that you should select the solution which has the fewest assumptions, as the more assumptions which you have to make, the more unlikely is that explanation.

I looked up from my notes at the fading afternoon settling in over Carluke. It had been an eventful day.

The boys moved on up the High Street, looking furtively around them all the time as they smoked, playing with their cigarettes in a private but also public way; they knew what they were doing was wrong, but they wanted to be seen nonetheless. They weren't ashamed of their smoking but seemed rather pleased by their transgression, laughing and joking and drawing attention to themselves. And, after all, what's the point of having transgressed if it is only you who knows that you have behaved badly? I've found in my work that people like their guilty secrets to become public, and they often invent bizarre ways of making that happen; the truth eventually spills out, like water from an overflowing bathtub. Even murderers behave like this and I thought again about Peter Manuel, who spent an extraordinary evening drinking with William Watt, claiming that he knew who had killed Watt's family. Of course he did – it was Manuel himself.

I watched the boys disappear from view, all the time aware that I had two hypotheses.

The first suggests that the killer had seen Margaret from his house, and as she made her way to the station he had left his house by his back door, which bordered the glen. He then entered the shortcut with the knife that he would use to kill her. Because he was able to observe what was going on in the street, he knew that there were no children playing outside. After he had killed Margaret he returned and disposed of the knife, cleaned himself and destroyed his bloody clothes.

The second hypothesis posits that her killer was returning home from work, and that he had spotted Margaret by chance in the street; that he carried a knife as part of his work (as the knife found at the crime scene was not the murder weapon); he was quick and efficient in his murder and was simply lucky that his attack went unobserved, and that there were no children playing in the glen; and, despite being covered in blood and undoubtedly emotionally high after achieving the kill, he was able to escape unnoticed.

When applying Occam's razor it becomes clear that the first

hypothesis is far more likely: it has the fewest assumptions and conforms to the rule of simplicity.

I stared at my notes, aware that this conclusion had left another question that I couldn't quite answer.

Why had there been no further murders?

My experience of this type of blitz-attack involving overkill is that the perpetrator does not simply stop, but will continue until he is caught and is imprisoned, moves away, is sectioned under the Mental Health Act, or perhaps commits suicide. Yet there were no further murders of this kind in Carluke until many years later, when in 2018 Quintus Montague killed his neighbour Paul Haley by stabbing him forty-seven times. If Muncie was alive I have no doubt that he would say that there were no further murders because the guilty party, George Beattie, had been locked up. That's not true, and so I needed to also determine why there was no other murder after Margaret's death.

I now had to think about other suspects.

There are numerous ways of answering my question as to why there were no further murders. If rumours in the town were to be believed, a more likely suspect had emigrated soon after Margaret's murder had been committed. Some said that he had gone to Australia, others to South Africa, but most were under the impression that he had moved to Canada. (It is likely that South Africa is another conflation, with people remembering that Margaret's fiancé had been working in South Africa at the time of her murder.) By far the most common reason given to me was that this suspect had moved to Canada; it was the story that the Bake House Café had repeated to me as well. If he had emigrated that would at least explain why there were no more killings in Carluke.

I had to interrogate where this information about Canada had come from, but also consider other explanations. I knew that I would have to find a way of answering all of this more definitively, although I wasn't yet in a position to do so. I looked again at my notes, hoping for inspiration. I read and re-read what I had written and I suddenly realised that part of the answer was staring me in the face – it had been obscured by my being so focused on trying to understand how the killer had managed to attack Margaret, and then escape undetected on the night of her death.

This attack *wasn't random*. It was targeted; he was killing her to save face. So after Margaret died her killer saw no *need* to kill again; he had done all that he wanted to do; he had, as he would have seen it, regained what he felt he had lost, or which he believed she had taken from him. Her death was all that he wanted to achieve. This wasn't an emerging serial killer I was profiling but simply a man who bore a dreadful, nonsensical, all-encompassing, life-changing, ill-conceived, murderous grudge against an innocent woman. This murder was about a personal obsession, and, through Margaret's death, her killer gained a form of release.

He had lost and then regained his control; he was disor- ganised and then organised. I wondered to what extent this dualism would be replicated in the killer's everyday life. Was he sick and suffering, but at the same time perhaps saw him- self as a 'superman'? Someone who was a cut above the rest?

Of course he still had to escape being detected after he had committed the murder and, while George's arrest took the police's attention away from him, how long would his luck last? He wasn't to know that George would be convicted and subsequently lose one appeal after another. He, perhaps in concert with his family, must have thought that he, or they, would have to act to keep his identity safe. Were they frightened that any day the police would come knocking at the door and his dreadful secret would be uncovered?

I am making assumptions here. I have no definitive way of knowing whether he acted with the knowledge and support of his family, and it is perfectly possible that they were unaware of what he had done. However, perhaps they were complicit in hiding his guilt from the police. This is not just speculation, even if I cannot prove it definitively. After all, Muncie told the newspapers: 'I feel sure some household must have noticed someone arriving home with signs of murder on his person. In kindness to that family, I appeal to them to come forward. It may well be that the killer needs attention and he could strike again.'

The family Muncie appealed to never came forward, but perhaps they had helped the actual killer to get the 'attention' he needed.

I closed my notebook. All of this was well and good as theorising, but I still had to come to some conclusion about who the killer might actually be.

*

That night Anne, Margaret, Willie and I went out for a meal at Prego in Clyde Street, near to the Bake House Café. We sat talking about our families, our various health issues – we are all getting to that age – and upcoming events when we would get together again. It was very pleasant, even if we had to occasionally shout to each other to overcome our mutual encroaching deafness. Afterwards I wanted to go to a pub and

Willie suggested the Railway Inn; he said that he didn't want to go to the Wee Thackit and I didn't push him as to why that might be. Anyway, the Railway Inn seemed to fit with the research that I had been conducting, given the importance of the railway to the story of Margaret's murder, and so we again made our way down Kirkton Street. We were soon settled and I noted the signs inside the pub banning football and uniform band colours after 8 p.m., as well as advertising the fact that Ricky Green was going to be there singing live. I did not know who Ricky Green was.

On the drinks menu was a 'Railway Cocktail' made of raspberry vodka, Chambord, cranberry juice, orange juice and lemonade – all for five pounds.

None of us were convinced.

We all eventually settled on something a little less exotic and sat down to continue our discussions.

There was a lull in the conversation and it was then that I took the opportunity to explain what I had been thinking about all day. I worry when I do this that I lose sight of the fact that most people don't really care about the issues I think are interesting. I become far too intense and clinical, and over time – often at the prompting of Anne – I have come to realise that some people can find this too dark and off-putting. It feels morbid to focus on the details of death in so casual a setting, especially after a lovely meal and over a quiet pint. Even so, Anne, Margaret and Willie listened silently as I explained what I had made of the murder site, and therefore my thinking in relation to her killer. I finished what I had to say and, a little embarrassed, looked into my near-empty beer glass.

It was Margaret who spoke.

'So,' she said, 'when are you going to tell us who it was?'

I just smiled by way of reply, drained my glass and asked if I could buy a round. I knew then that I would have to start to firm up and try to conclude my research.

I owed this to Margaret McLaughlin, to George Beattie, and to Carluke.

CHAPTER EIGHT

Other Suspects

'He said it might have been him,
might not have been him'

T he conclusion of my criminological autopsy and my
emerging hypothesis meant that I needed to know much
more about the people who had been living in Unitas Crescent
at the time. Which men in the street might have been in the
age range that will typically kill? Who lived in the houses that
bordered the shortcut to the station and had back doors and
gardens on to the glen? Who might have found it cathartic
to have killed Margaret? To build up a picture of who had
been resident there in 1973, I consulted the electoral roll for
Carluke from the early 1970s.

In total, forty-two people were recorded as living in 108
to 74 Unitas Crescent, the row of houses where I believed
that Margaret's killer must have resided, based on my profile
and criminological autopsy. However, this number included

women. As the killer was undoubtedly male, I could immediately bring the number down to twenty. This gender
specification makes criminological sense – murder really is a
young man's business. Year after year, for every ten murders
that get committed nine will have been perpetrated by men,
and these men will be disproportionately young and from
lower socioeconomic classes. This general gender pattern
in relation to murder is so well established that it is perhaps
the closest that criminology has ever come to establishing a
'fact' about crime. We can also infer gender by the nature of
the attack – it was bloody and violent and in such a frenzy
that Margaret was unable to successfully defend herself. Her
dead body was also moved, which would require a degree
of strength.

These assumptions allowed me to narrow down my list of
suspects, although before I could consider them further I was
offered three more names of potential suspects, none of whom
lived in Unitas Crescent.

I was quickly able to discount these suggestions. The first
name I received was John Hall, a small-time thief and drug
dealer from Carluke who was shot dead in a professional
underworld hit in 2001. Hall was regarded by the first of my
correspondents as 'a bit weird and a loner', but he had stuck
in their heads as a likely suspect as he had worn a top hat
with mirrors on it to a disco in the town shortly after George
had been convicted. This is indeed strange and insensitive
behaviour, but Hall never lived in Unitas Crescent and his
criminal career was that of a petty offender who by and large
sold drugs. Indeed, he seems to have been killed because he
owed £120,000 for a cocaine deal that had gone wrong; he had

been trying to move up an organised criminal hierarchy and it hadn't worked out. There was no interpersonal violence that I could uncover in his offending history, and when it comes to the mirrored hat, well, sadly people are cruel and insensitive about murder more often than one would expect.

I rejected the other two suggestions because the first had no connection to Margaret that I could find, and did not live in Unitas Crescent. Also, my email correspondent revealed that they had only suggested his name as they had 'an uneasy feeling' about this individual, which is a very weak basis on which to build a case. The final person suggested by email did not live in Carluke at all, and I could find nothing that would have put him at the scene of the murder.

As with these last two unidentified suspects, it would also be unfair to name the men on my list of twenty who constituted the pool of Unitas Crescent residents that I began to focus my research on. I soon discovered that three of these twenty had been formally interviewed by the police, but released without charge – they all had alibis. This reduced the pool to seventeen. As I have indicated, murder is a young man's business and so I believed that Margaret's killer would be a male of voting age, but it would be unlikely for him to have been over forty. Based on my profile of how this murder was committed, by the age of forty the perpetrator would have already acquired a criminal record and so would have left his mark on official documents such as court reports. However, I found none which were relevant. There would also have been local intelligence about a man who was in his thirties or forties, which I felt my Bake House Café sounding board would have known all about. I did not think it likely, again based on criminological research, that Margaret's murderer was below voting age. Using all of these assumptions and excluding the three men who had alibis, I was able to reduce my list of other suspects to three.

I have no doubt that at least one of these men should have been fully investigated by the police in connection with Margaret's murder. In trying to narrow down these three suspects, I was helped by some old-fashioned research.

George Beattie's case regularly featured in various Scottish newspapers and so I also consulted these, sometimes online if the newspapers had digitised their archives, or in the British Library if they had not. I noticed that over the years these newspapers, though never actively campaigning on behalf of George, began to describe his case as 'controversial', especially after his lawyers lodged successive appeals. I read the reports of these various appeals and the relevant edition of Hansard, for when Jimmy Hood, the local MP, made an impassioned plea on George's behalf in the House of Commons in March 1993. It was partly in response to Hood's coruscating attack on George's conviction that the case was referred back to the Scottish Appeal Court, where matters then came to a head in late 1994. By March the following year George had been released on licence, although he has never been exonerated.

I was reading about these various twists and turns of the case when I came across an article in the *Glasgow Herald*, published on 30 March 1995, reporting on an appeal lodged on behalf of George. The article described how two former detective constables in the Scottish Crime Squad called Ian Muir and Bob Beveridge had interviewed a man that they thought was a much more likely suspect than George Beattie.

Muir and Beveridge had been seconded from their normal duties to help with door-to-door enquiries in Carluke a few days after Margaret's body had been found, as the local police didn't have sufficient resources to do all of the enquiries themselves. Beveridge is quoted as saying that a suspect

> more or less jumped up from the settee, and without any prompting he said it might have been him [that committed the murder]. He then turned up his jersey and showed me what he claimed were stab wounds on his chest and lower abdomen.

Beveridge described how they took this unnamed suspect into custody for further questioning. While detained at Carluke Police Station, he revealed more about himself. In his notes Muir wrote, 'one of the strange things he did say was that his pastime was going round the neighbourhood stabbing cats – quite disturbing comments from a disturbing guy ... he later told me he took great delight in stabbing cats. Obviously he was quite used to knives.' Despite all of this, the officers were told to let him go, because George Beattie had just been charged with Margaret's murder.

It was an extraordinary discovery.

This suspect clearly fitted many aspects of the profile that I had been developing. He used knives and was sufficiently odd to be described as 'disturbing' by two experienced detectives, which implied he had underlying mental health issues. He also had stab wounds on his chest. Might these have been caused by Margaret when she fought back during the attack? Could she have pushed his knife away from her and towards the body of her killer? His 'jumping' from the settee might also be seen as evidence that he was still emotionally high and disinhibited in those very early days after committing the murder, and, most concerning of all, it is stated that he spoke to the police, and suggested that he 'might' indeed have been the culprit.

Who was this suspect? No name was given in the article, only descriptions of what he had said and how he had behaved.

Where in the town had Beveridge and Muir conducted their enquiries and where exactly had they encountered this suspect? Could it have been Unitas Crescent and, if so, where exactly?

I needed to make contact with the two detectives to follow up on this lead – the best I'd had yet – as it took me to the heart of the police's investigation in July 1973.

As far as I was concerned, this man had moved to the top of my list to become the primary suspect for Margaret's murder and trying to discover his identity quickly became a focus for my research. I still had my three suspects from sifting through the electoral register, but my priority was now trying to put a name to Beveridge and Muir's man. With this suspect there was some solid empirical evidence to investigate, and perhaps much more to go on than his simply having lived on the relevant street. I felt I'd found my first real lead. Whatever the gossip in the town might have been about the person responsible, here was evidence from two detectives who were prepared to go on record about what had taken place during the investigation in 1973, and to describe a 'disturbing guy' they had encountered, but whom they had been told to release without him being fully investigated. I wasn't relying on statistical probability here, but had real, tangible evidence about the personality and behaviour of an individual who had been brought in for questioning at the time.

Beveridge and Muir's suspect had explained that he carried a knife because it was his 'pastime' to stab cats in the neighbourhood, and that he got a great deal of delight from doing so. This was interesting from a number of perspectives, but first we should consider why some people, such as the man encountered by the two detectives, deliberately harm animals and question whether, if they do this as a child or as an adolescent, this type of behaviour is an important indicator for predicting violent criminal behaviour when they mature? If Beveridge and Muir's suspect had been in his twenties or thirties – in other words, after he had already matured – and was stabbing cats because this had become his 'pastime', it suggested that they had been in the presence of a very dangerous and violent man.

I needed to find out who this man was; and perhaps, just perhaps, what if it transpired that he was one of my own three suspects?

That really would be astonishing.

*

However, given what Beveridge and Muir are quoted as saying about their suspect, I want to pause a moment and think about men who use violence towards animals. In recent years, and certainly since the 1970s, there has been renewed interest in understanding why some people are cruel to animals. Known academically as intentional animal torture and cruelty (IATC), the recent interest in the subject is perhaps due to the media interest in the case of the so-called 'Croydon Cat Killer'. The Croydon Cat Killer was thought to have killed, dismembered and decapitated over four hundred cats across England, beginning in Croydon in 2014. This is where he gained his moniker, but there seemed to be a pattern of similar attacks on cats in various towns and cities around the M25 motorway, and reaching as far north as the town of Northampton.

In 2018, after spending nearly £130,000 and over two thousand hours on the case, the Metropolitan Police concluded that the killing of the cats in Croydon had been carried out by wildlife – most probably urban foxes – or by their scavenging on the cats after they had been run over by traffic.

However, when it came to Northampton, a thirty-two-year-old man called Brendan Gaughan was convicted of killing and mutilating seven cats. He was sentenced to three years in prison.

Gaughan was also a prolific arsonist, and cruelty to animals and fire-setting have been seen since the 1960s as two of the three components – the final one being bed-wetting – of a 'homicidal triad' in adolescents proposed by the forensic psychiatrist J. M. Macdonald. Though there has been little empirical support for the triad as a predictive tool, it is still of interest that a number of serial or multiple murderers, such as Jeffrey Dahmer, had indeed been cruel to animals in their youth. In fact, our current diagnostic criteria for childhood conduct disorder and anti-social personality disorder would still include animal cruelty and deliberate fire-setting as two of a cluster of at least ten other factors, some of the others being lying, stealing, playing truant, destroying property and breaking into cars or homes. Whatever the resulting behaviours, IATC in adolescence remains a serious issue, as it can indicate antisocial tendencies that may continue into adulthood.

In court Gaughan claimed that he had killed the first two cats out of 'spite' and that he had gained 'satisfaction' from killing the others. He would leave the dismembered bodies of the cats on the cars or in the gardens of their owners. He also admitted to having had other violent thoughts and fantasies, including of entering women's houses and raping and then killing them. This move from killing animals to killing humans is sometimes called the 'species jump' and is one of the reasons why the FBI in particular have been keen to endorse the homicidal triad, as they see this cluster of factors in the backgrounds of many serial killers.

In his defence, Gaughan's barrister said that he was 'a man with mental health issues. [He] feels isolated and vulnerable in the community in which he lives.' I wondered to what extent this defence might also echo the life and circumstances of the man I was searching for in Carluke.

However, there are a number of other reasons why people engage in this type of behaviour. For some it is a way of gaining revenge, or a means by which they can coerce, control or intimidate female partners or children to be silent about abuse. In those cases, the perpetrator would attack a beloved pet – or threaten to do so – if the victim suggested that they were going to reveal what had been happening to them. To attack or threaten the pet has a number of advantages for the abuser. It leaves no mark on human victims (which might attract attention) and can be easily explained away as that the pet simply having got into a fight with another animal.

Brendan Gaughan was not an adolescent when he killed and dismembered the seven cats in Northampton. Yet his underlying mental health issues and his fantasies about raping and killing women are eerily reminiscent of what Muir and Beveridge said about the man that they discovered. Their account of him suggests a man with an acute antisocial personality and someone, like Gaughan, who probably had difficulties in the community and so felt isolated and vulnerable.

But who was this suspect and where exactly in Carluke had Muir and Beveridge undertaken their house-to-house enquiries? What if they had been knocking on doors in Unitas Crescent? Did they perhaps encounter the man who many people in the town thought was a much more likely suspect than George Beattie? If they had, and this was indeed the disturbing and odd suspect that they described in the press, it would transform my research from dealing with what people suspected at the time to providing concrete evidence that would push my investigation forward.

Of course, before I could ask any of my questions I had to track down Muir and Beveridge.

*

It is said that we now exist in and through social media. Ever since the 1990s, when the internet escaped from the academy and entered everyday life, social networking sites, content-sharing platforms, net-enabled mobile phones and video calling have begun to change the way that we present ourselves to the world, and how we communicate with one another. It seems that most of us want to tell our personal story as publicly as possible. This is sometimes known as having 'mediated visibility'. To be is to be seen, and people now carve out ever more creative ways of establishing a public space for the 'self' – not just on Facebook or Twitter, but through blogs or personal webpages. These public selves are usually the ones that we would prefer other people to see, as opposed to our often less glamorous private reality. We can even achieve this from the phones we carry around in our pockets.

Murderers are no exception.

My colleague Professor Elizabeth Yardley and I studied forty-eight homicide cases in which the murderer had used Facebook. We found that murderers used Facebook in six different ways and labelled these killers as reactors, informers, antagonists, fantasists, predators and impostors. Reactors responded to content that had been posted on Facebook by their partner, ex-partner or would-be partner by attacking the victim offline and face-to-face. The content may have been posted online and the killer would immediately react to what he had viewed, or he might wait for some time to pass and continually revisit Facebook and the content, ruminating over what it might mean for their relationship. On the other hand, antagonists would engage in hostile exchanges online until these escalated into face-to-face violence, often after the antagonist had been able to arm himself with a weapon.

Social media has become so embedded in our lives that it is commonplace for the police to use social media, phone records and all our other networked technology to build up a picture of who a murder victim was, and their circle of family, friends and work colleagues, and in doing so get a better picture of their likely murderer. As generations of research have shown, people are usually murdered by someone they know.

At a more mundane level, we can now construct a biographical picture of people we might never have met, or have only just recently been introduced to, simply through using social media sites, or by typing their name into an internet search engine. In just a few seconds I can discover a great deal about a person, and I have grown to rather distrust people who don't have any kind of electronic footprint. *What is it*, I find myself thinking, *that they've got to hide? Why are they 'invisible' and what is it exactly that they don't want to be seen?*

I first typed both 'Robert Beveridge' and 'Bob Beveridge' into my search engine, as I felt that it was a more unusual name than 'Ian Muir'. There were a number of 'Beveridges' that had to be sifted through, but only one was in the correct age range and who had had a policing background.

Quite quickly I was able to track down Bob Beveridge, as he had often given interviews to the Scottish press about his career, and then his later decision to leave the police.

It's always amazing, the picture that I can build from an online search. I discovered that Bob had been born in 1942, in Kingskettle, a small village in Fife, and that his family had once owned a linen factory. When he was eleven, Bob's family had inherited a rather grand house in the village called The Poplars and, on taking possession of the house, they discovered there all kinds of old violins, violas and cellos. Bob had been allowed to keep them for himself, and so began a lifelong interest in string instruments. He studied at Dundee Art College then, aged nineteen, he had joined the Fife Police and soon afterwards became a detective. He was seconded to the Scottish Crime Squad, which at one time was based in Edinburgh, but his work took him all over Scotland. He left the police in 1977 and, in an interview that he gave to the *Courier* in January 2018, explained what had prompted that decision:

One Sunday morning Bob was working in the identification bureau with Glasgow CID when he was called to the police mortuary to fingerprint three murder victims. One had been stabbed, the second shot and the third had been kicked to death after a farewell party.

That grim scene, coming soon after Bob had to photograph the charred remains of three boys after a house fire, convinced him that working seven days a week sometimes nearly 24 hours a day was not for him or his family.

Bob returned to his love of musical instruments and set up a violin shop in Falkland, which he runs to this day. His expertise in this area has meant that he has been a member of the expert panel on *Antiques Roadshow* – quite a change from the life of a detective.

This biography of Bob that I have described is the type of information that I now routinely expect to be able to discover through social media and online records. Within a matter of minutes I can create a picture of a complete stranger that previously would have taken me weeks or months of research. There is an obvious danger in relying solely on what is recorded online, as this can often have been manipulated for personal advantage. I therefore still tend to favour old-fashioned paper archives and what I can discover in libraries, and use the information that I find there to develop, or confirm what I might have discovered online.

It was easy to find a contact number for Bob's violin shop, and from there I was given Bob's mobile phone number. He was happy to speak to me and quite quickly revealed that Ian Muir had died several years ago. Though I was keen to find out as much as I could from Bob, I didn't want to 'lead the witness', as they would say in a court of law, about the suspect that he had encountered. In our first conversation I let Bob guide me as to his memories – although he self-deprecatingly warned me not to expect too much as he was nearly eighty years old. What follows is a transcript of our first conversation, edited slightly to remove pauses and other extraneous details:

DW: Can you tell me a little more about the person that you and Ian Muir questioned on your house-to-house enquiries that you described in the *Glasgow Herald*?

BB: It didn't take us long to get on to this chap through our house-to-house enquiries. He was in his twenties. He was average build and quite well dressed. He had dark hair – definitely not blond or ginger. Not bad looking. He didn't say an awful lot, but he did know Margaret McLaughlin – they all seemed to, as it was a close-knit community. Thinking about it, it was what he didn't say that was so interesting, because he showed no interest in the girl having been murdered. He expressed no remorse.

DW: Did he mention employment?

BB: No – he didn't say anything about that.

DW: How long were you and Ian in his company?

BB: From eight in the evening until nine the next morning at the police station in Carluke. We were always awake and we played cards and dominoes. It was all very casual and he never made any protest about being detained. He had a lot of bravado and seemed to be quite happy in our company.

DW: Do you remember his name?

BB: No. It's so long ago now. I can't remember what he was called. I don't have access to my old police notebooks.

DW: How did cats enter the conversation?

BB: He rolled up his jumper and said he'd recently been stabbed. This was when we were doing the house-to-house enquiries. To me the wounds looked quite superficial – perhaps even self-inflicted – and they certainly didn't need hospital treatment. He then said he'd been stabbing cats in the local area and that he got pleasure out of it – that's why he carried a knife.

DW: He carried a knife about with him?

BB: Yes, that's what he said. I said, 'You make it a habit to carry a knife around with you?' He said that he did because he liked to stab the cats. You know yourself how that might progress to stabbing people.

DW: Did you also ask if he had killed Margaret McLaughlin?

BB: We did.

DW: What did he say to that?

BB: He said, 'I might have; I don't remember what I did yesterday.' Quite off the cuff. He just wasn't prepared to talk about the murder at all. He was really odd. We thought that he'd had some involvement but I could never say that he was guilty. He needed to be eliminated from the enquiries, but we were then told to let him go. It all struck me as odd.

DW: Do you think that his cuts could have been the result of Margaret fighting back?

BB: Well, that's possible too.

DW: What else do you remember about him?

BB: Just that I had never met a character like him and I had done hundreds of murder enquiries. He was a bit of a nutter. He should have been eliminated from the investigation – him and the boyfriend that she used to have.

It might be helpful here to clarify what Bob means by 'eliminated from the investigation'. He wanted his suspect to be looked at more closely, and for the police to have checked his offending background, his movements on the night that Margaret was murdered, and to have tested any alibi that he might have offered. None of that happened because by then Muncie was focussed on George Beattie.

I was keen to continue our conversation but I didn't want to push Bob too much, having just made contact. Instead, I thanked Bob for talking to me, checked if it would be all right if I called him again if I had any further questions, and gave him my contact details. I was hoping that this initial conversation would spark some memories and wanted him to be able to get in touch. I sat down to think about what I had asked; what I didn't ask and what I might want to ask the next time we spoke; and once again tried to make sense of everything that I had been told so far.

As it turned out, it would be Bob who contacted me first.

**

This initial discussion with Bob was effectively a repetition of the story that he had first revealed in the *Glasgow Herald*. That gave me confidence that he hadn't exaggerated in the course of a rather high-profile and controversial appeal. The story that he told me over twenty years later contained all of the original elements: the strange suspect who had been controversially let go; how this suspect had been in the habit of carrying a knife, a knife which he said he used to stab cats; the marks on his abdomen; and finally the fact that he should have been eliminated from enquiries, rather than simply being released from custody. However, there were also new and added details that are worth considering too. Above all else, Bob had offered a physical description of the suspect, which he hadn't done in his press interview. This man was in his twenties and had dark hair – he was definitely not blond, or red-headed. He was of average build and not bad looking. This information would prove extremely helpful in confirming my shortlist that I made from the pool of twenty suspects in Unitas Crescent, though I hadn't asked Bob where, specifically, he had conducted his door-to-door enquiries, or suggested any names to him. I was trying to be scrupulously fair – I had to keep an open mind and allow the evidence to guide me, rather than imposing my analysis from the criminological autopsy and profile on the people I interviewed. Even so, Bob's description that he and Ian were working within a 'close-knit community' where everyone knew Margaret implied at the very least that they were conducting enquiries in the housing schemes either in or surrounding Glenburn Terrace or Unitas Crescent.

Bob also confirmed that this suspect did indeed know Margaret, even if he hadn't expressed remorse about her murder. This helped me to think about this suspect's state of mind just days after the murder – why wasn't he remorseful? Perhaps he was pleased that she was dead. Or perhaps he had such disordered thinking that he didn't realise how serious the situation actually was, which was why Bob described the suspect's comments as being 'off the cuff'. I thought again about Bob's observation that everyone knew Margaret because it was a 'close-knit community' and heard in his statement echoes of the research that I had conducted about Facebook murderers, even though there had been no such thing at the time. Margaret's killer could have been functioning like a Facebook reactor, responding to what she had been doing and with whom she had formed a relationship. When Bob asked directly if he had killed Margaret, he had replied 'I might have; I don't remember what I did yesterday.' In other words, he didn't deny that he was responsible for her death; he was controlled and, at the same time, disorganised in his thinking.

Why might this man not have been able to remember what he had done the day before? Was this a stalling device, or should we take what he said at face value? Did he not remember because of medication he was taking? After all, if he was odd enough to be described as 'a bit of a nutter' and the most extraordinary character in all of the murder enquiries that Bob had conducted, it does not seem unreasonable to conclude that he had mental health problems.

I also wondered if this suspect had been questioned under caution, or if Bob and Ian just brought him in for further questioning at the police station. Unlike George, he does not appear to have been formally interviewed, which was why Bob and Ian had stayed up all night with him playing cards and dominoes and engaging in general conversation. He was not subjected to the same pressures that George was placed under.

This seemed odd to me. Why had they not arrested their suspect and then formally interviewed him? And if he *hadn't* been arrested, why did the suspect willingly go to the police station?

I was still trying to make sense of all of this, and had begun to feel like I'd reached a bit of a road block, when a few days after our first interview, Bob wrote to me. I eagerly opened the envelope. His letter had his address and a picture of his shop in Falkland in the top right-hand corner, and in blue ink he told me about the weather in Fife. He apologised for being unable to remember the name of the suspect and lamented the death of his former colleague Ian Muir. There was a 'PTO' at the bottom of the page. On the other side of the letter he had drawn a crude map of the houses where he and Ian had been posted to conduct their house-to-house enquiries and also where, as he wrote on his map, 'I seem to recall [we met] the suspect'.

The map was of the houses that bordered the gap in Unitas Crescent which Margaret would have used as her shortcut to the railway station.

Bob even identified specific houses where he thought that he might have encountered the suspect that had so astonished him. He didn't number these houses on his map – clearly he couldn't remember this type of detail and nor did he draw the houses as if they were semi-detached – but I was aware from what he had drawn that he had identified numbers 80 and 78 Unitas Crescent on one side of the gap that created the shortcut, and 76, 74 and 72 Unitas Crescent on the other.

It is hard to express how I felt at that moment, but I looked at Bob's map for several minutes as if it was some sort of precious object, carefully turning his letter over in my hands. I took a breath and cautiously placed it on my desk, smoothing out the rough edges of the paper.

This was a real breakthrough moment; this was progress.

However, I believed that 72 Unitas Crescent would have been too far away for the suspect to have known who was playing in the grassy area, and was, in any case, occupied by an elderly married couple in 1973. Number 74 had a sole female occupant, which left one man living at 76 and the male occupants of numbers 78 and 80 on the other side of the gap.

I had already reduced my twenty suspects to three, and now I felt that I was coming closer to reducing that number even further, by being able to put a name to the 'bit of a nutter' whom Bob and Ian had encountered.

Bob's letter was a shock to my system. After all these years I was getting closer to the truth about the identity of a much more likely suspect, who should have been ruled out of the police investigation.

I phoned Bob and, given that the information he'd offered to me was given without my prompting, I felt able to ask more direct questions without 'leading the witness'. Even so, I deliberately framed some of my questions so that I was offering a number of different outcomes, any of which Bob might have chosen.

DW: The houses that you draw on the map relate to
the gap in Unitas Crescent – the shortcut to the

station – which is between numbers 80/78 and
76/74; they're semi-detached houses.

BB: I don't remember the numbers, but Ian and I were
designated the task of doing the house-to-house
enquiries on that small group of houses.

DW: That's OK, but I was just wondering could you have
encountered the suspect on the other side of the
gap – at numbers 80/78?

[Pause]

BB: Ah, certainly when you mention the number 80, I
wouldn't rule that out as that may well have been
the house where we found our suspect. But, because
of the passage of time, I just can't be 100 per
cent certain.

I noted, but did not make any comment at the time, that
Bob had mentioned number 80 but not 78.

It was, I felt, time to suggest names for the suspect that
they had encountered. I didn't want to come right out and
say whom I thought they had interviewed, no matter how
tempting it might have been, but instead offered Bob a choice
of names based on who I knew was living in Unitas Crescent
at the time, mixed with some completely random names.
In all I suggested five names, including those of the man
widely believed to have been a more credible suspect than
George Beattie, and of an elderly man who lived in one of the
houses that Bob had identified, and waited expectantly for
Bob's answer.

I was to be disappointed. Bob really couldn't remember
what the suspect was called.

Even so, our discussions had pushed forward my research in a number of different ways. What he had told me really did suggest that the suspect they had encountered was living in the high even-numbered houses of Unitas Crescent, and specifically was living in one of the houses that bordered the shortcut to the railway station. He had been unable to confirm a house number, or give a name for the suspect, although he could not rule out the possibility that he had encountered him at 80 Unitas Crescent. This gave me confidence that the profile that I had constructed at the start of the research was on the right lines and that my criminological autopsy had also been accurate.

It also gave me a new problem.

Should I reveal what Bob had told me to my sisters and the Bake House Café sounding board? I was hesitant as I didn't want what we had discussed to imply that I had solved the 'mystery' of who might have killed Margaret, nor did I want what he had revealed to seep out from the café into the town. I still had research to do before I felt that I would be able to demonstrate anything more empirically.

But, on balance, I took the view that my approach so far had been to be as open as possible and that approach had paid dividends. Why change that now?

I'm glad that I didn't change my methodology, because what I learned from our next discussion completely transformed the course of my research.

*

We next gathered in the Bake House Café in March 2019, before I gave a talk at Carluke Library. Everyone was there except for Annie, and before we had finished talking we were also joined by my nephew Paul. I slowly went through what Bob had said and Margaret, Alison, Maureen, Laura and Margo listened in silence as I edged towards telling them that when he had been a detective he and a colleague had conducted house-to-house enquiries in Unitas Crescent. I described the extraordinary suspect that Bob and Ian had encountered, but kept back the physical description. Everything that I said was news to them. That in itself was of interest, as it suggested that local intelligence at the time and their memories of the events of July 1973 could only take me so far. I explained how this suspect had told the detectives that he had carried a knife with him because he enjoyed stabbing cats in the local area.

Laura and Margo looked confused.

I asked them if they remembered cats being attacked around the time of Margaret's murder. Neither of them did and I quickly reasoned that if there had been, they would surely have known all about it. More than this, pets would have been disappearing more often than usual and eventually corpses of cats would be found in the undergrowth, or lying out in the open.

It became clear that this man wasn't attacking cats with a knife that he was in the habit of carrying. Perhaps he was fantasising about doing so, or simply finding an excuse to explain why the knife was in his possession, and for the marks on his abdomen. Later it struck me that I didn't really understand why the man had shown them to Bob and Ian at all. If he hadn't lifted up his jumper, the detectives would have been none the wiser. Was this a guilty secret finding a bizarre way to be made public? As with the boys smoking in the street, or Peter Manuel spending a night drinking with the husband and the father of the women that he had mur-dered, what's the point of transgressing if no one else knows that you have done so?

I then described the houses that Bob had drawn on his crude map; which numbers these equated to; and how during our subsequent telephone conversation he had suggested to me that he couldn't rule out that he and Ian had met their suspect at number 80 Unitas Crescent.

There was a perceptible change in the atmosphere when I mentioned this address, as if the air was being sucked out of the place. The café's characteristic warmth had abruptly become chilly.

I knew why.

I had realised, from studying the electoral roll, that this was the house where the man who was widely suspected in the town as being a more credible suspect than George Beattie lived – as did almost everyone else sitting around the table in the Bake House Café.

I let this information sink in, but I wanted to move on before they started to talk amongst themselves about what I had just said. I still had other questions that I wanted to pursue with the sounding board and I needed to ask these in much the same way that I had questioned Bob. Even if all of the information I was sharing pointed in one direction, I wanted them to confirm or deny facts without me leading them to any specific answer. Perhaps, for example, they would say that this man had blond or red hair – while Bob had spe-cifically described him as having dark hair.

I asked them if they could share their general memories of this man as a way of starting the discussion.

Laura remembered that he was 'so quiet – you never really saw him'.

'Why was that?' I asked.

'I thought that he was a swot,' Laura explained. 'He was older than us and I just thought he was clever and was always studying, which was why we never saw him.'

Margo added more detail: 'You didn't see him too often and when you did he always came across as preoccupied. He didn't seem to have a social group; he didn't seem to be out and about in the street.'

This information is of great interest, especially as it came from Laura and Margo unprompted by me. This man was 'quiet', 'you didn't see him too often' and 'he didn't seem to have a social group', even though this was a close-knit community, where people knew one another's business. He was therefore different from George Beattie, whom everyone seemed to know and therefore was all too noticeable. Laura and Margo put the lack of visibility of the man at number 80 down to his being a 'swot', and by implication being in his room reading rather outside socialising with people of a similar age. Was that necessarily true? Might there have been other reasons why he didn't have a social group, why he appeared to be preoccupied, or to explain why people didn't see him in the town too often?

Being a recluse does not, of course, make you an offender; there are many people who simply prefer their own company. However, being isolated and not living within a social group does allow an individual to avoid the demands of social convention and behaving in ways that are expected. Even so, I had to be careful not to just accept the sounding board's views uncritically and to keep in mind that they had always harboured suspicions about him.

I asked if they could offer a physical description of this man and both Laura and Margo smiled. 'He was handsome,' said Laura, and Margo added for good measure, 'You'd look twice at him.' Again this felt significant, given that Bob had said that he was 'not bad looking', but I pushed for something more tangible, rather than subjective. After all, what is handsome to one person might not be for another. I was trying hard not to give away my own suspicions – all the information had to come from them, without being planted by me. Just like in any good police interview, I didn't want to be leading the witness.

It was Laura who spoke first. 'I remember that he was tall and had dark hair.'

It wasn't much, but it fitted well enough. Even though Bob had described the suspect as being of 'average' build, Laura could easily, and understandably, have remembered him as being tall, as she was a child and this man was in his twenties. But it was the colour of his hair that was important. This man was not blond or red-headed, but dark – just like the person that Bob and Ian had encountered, in exactly the same area that they had been conducting house-to-house enquiries and about whom people in the town – behind closed doors – were suggesting as a far more plausible suspect than George.

This was a tipping point, and I started to reduce my list of Unitas Crescent suspects to one.

But there was another huge revelation to come.

I was sipping at my coffee, listening to the conversation going on beside me, when, almost as an aside, Laura commented that this man was the ex-boyfriend of Margaret's, and that she had broken up with him. She added, 'I remember most of the women in the crescent saying it was more likely to be him [she names a suspect] than poor George. They said that because she [Margaret] had left him and then he just disappeared after the murder.'

I sat there for a few seconds, processing what I had just heard. 'She'd left him'; Margaret had been in a relationship with this man. This was news to me, but it confirmed what I had written in my original profile. I thought at that time that Margaret's killer had been obsessional and that her death had been a form of cathartic release. This new information seemed to suggest a much deeper and more anguished relationship with Margaret, and so threw further light on the man whom Bob and Ian had interviewed. Things were starting to slot into place – like the pieces of a jigsaw which, when put together, allow the whole picture to emerge.

Unbeknownst to Bob and Ian, the man they had discovered in Unitas Crescent, the man with whom they had played cards and dominoes the whole night, the suspect who 'might' have been responsible for Margaret's death, was, if Laura's memory is correct, an ex-boyfriend (who he obviously thought was another person altogether) whom she had rejected before becoming engaged to her fiancé. That they did not discover this at the time is either an indication of how little their suspect had revealed to them (he was controlled once again), or the inaccurate product of Laura's memory. Whom should we believe?

There are clues to that answer even in what the suspect said to Bob. He was silent and uncommunicative about Margaret, which was the very thing that had made Bob suspicious of him – 'It was what he didn't say that was so interesting.' The suspect did not express surprise about Margaret's murder, nor did he show any sorrow about her death. All in all, 'he wasn't prepared to talk about the murder at all'. Bob could not have guessed just how true that statement rang in his discussion with me, as I knew from his map that he had undoubtedly been in the company of the man whom everyone in the town thought was a much more likely suspect than George. I am left with the impression that the last thing he would have wanted to do while playing cards or dominoes with the two detectives was to admit that he had in fact been in a relationship with Margaret. Frankly, I would trust Laura's memory.

I was at first confused as to why people in the town did not know that this suspect had spent the night at the police station, but I later came to realise that the arrest and then charging of George had deflected attention away from him and onto George as the 'culprit'. What was happening to George became the focus of everyone's attention. It was this suspect's good fortune that George's arrest turned attention away from him – a good fortune that had lasted for a very long time.

*

Given that all of this information had emerged in a short space of time, I knew it was important for me to take stock and carefully consider the evidence that had emerged, and the order in which it had done so.

There had always been an open secret that people believed someone else was a much more likely suspect. I knew this person's name, but I did not know exactly where he had lived – indeed I had never actually been in Unitas Crescent before undertaking my criminological autopsy – or what he might have looked like. I knew very little of his personal history. I constructed a profile of the likely killer at the very earliest stages of my research, based on my experience of using investigative psychology in cold and live cases. I constructed that profile with the barest of knowledge of the information which would emerge during my Bake House Café sounding boards – all that I knew for certain was this suspect's name. I had not at that stage been to the murder site and therefore didn't understand the specific geography of the killing.

I want to be fair in this process and so I must state that my focus on this man does not prove that he is the guilty party. More research would need to be done before I could even begin to attempt to prove that the police should have regarded him as a prime suspect in Margaret's murder. But there was also more that I could do. Specifically, I wanted to track this suspect down and, if he was still alive, interview him and put to him what I have discovered to see how he might answer these charges. He might have perfectly reasonable explanations for what I had discovered and for the statements that he made to Bob and Ian. It is conceivable that he left the town simply to escape the rumours and gossip circulating about him. We should also remember that people who have mental health problems are far more likely to harm themselves, rather than other people, and I have already drawn attention to why some people falsely claim to have been the perpetrator of a murder, or to claim that they 'might' have been.

My criminological autopsy allowed me to see Unitas Crescent and Glenburn Terrace come to life, and in turn being in the murder site also enabled me to test aspects of my profile of the killer. I identified the houses where I believed that Margaret's killer would live. Through consulting the electoral roll for Carluke for the early 1970s I was able to put names to the addresses of those living in those streets at the time of Margaret's murder.

My archival research concerning George Beattie's appeal in the 1990s yielded Bob Beveridge's statement in the *Glasgow Herald* about his conducting house-to-house enquiries in Carluke and how he had encountered a suspect he thought was a 'bit of a nutter'. It was only through tracking down and then interviewing Bob that I was able to establish that he had been tasked with conducting his enquiries in a small group of houses in Carluke. It didn't take long to realise that he was describing those houses in Unitas Crescent which bordered the gap that formed the shortcut that Margaret would have taken on her fateful journey to the station.

In other words, the man widely believed in the town to be a more likely suspect was undoubtedly the odd interviewee who stated that he 'might' have killed Margaret that Bob and Ian had encountered. It was coincidence, the combination of research, Bob's testimony and the combined knowledge of the Bake House Café that brought me to this understanding.

I did not create this coincidence; it emerged from documents and interviews.

The key person in all of this is of course Bob Beveridge. He is an independent witness; someone who comes with no local or indeed historical axe to grind. Bob knew nothing of the gossip that was circulating at the time, or of the suspicions of the Bake House Café – suspicions that I can legitimately be accused of being party to at the time, as well as more recently.

Weighing all of this up, it now feels right to give a name to this suspect. I can do so only by giving him an assumed name, but, of course, if the police ever want to re-open this case all of my research is available to them. I also want to identify this suspect so that I do not bring unwanted suspicion on any other individuals who might have been mentioned to me during the course of my research. It was also at this stage of my research that I started the process of attempting to track this suspect down to see if he would be willing to talk to me. I did not know if I would find him in a grave, or happily living in another country.

CHAPTER NINE

In Search of 'John Smith'

'He came across as preoccupied'

John Smith lived with his parents and his sister at 80 Unitas Crescent, Carluke. He was born at the William Smellie Maternity Hospital in Lanark in January 1949, and his father's occupation was listed on the birth certificate as 'company cashier', although there's no information on what company that might have been. I asked Laura and Margo about Smith's family and they described them as being 'very reserved and respected' and, beyond this natural reserve, perhaps his father's managerial, white-collar occupation had also set the family apart from other people living in Unitas Crescent, who were mostly employed at the steel works or in similar blue-collar jobs.

In July 1973 Smith was twenty-four years old. I couldn't find out if he was employed or unemployed at the time. However, I did know that both he and his sister had passed the 11-plus exam and so had gone to the grammar school, Wishaw High, rather than the local comprehensive. This was no doubt why Laura and Margo remember Smith as being 'clever' and 'a bit of a swot'.

My eldest sister, Alison, had also gone to Wishaw High, though she was several years younger than Smith. Nonetheless she remembered an incident on a school trip in Europe when he had had some kind of nervous breakdown that had resulted in his parents having to come and collect him. Margo and Laura also remembered the incident when I raised it with them – perhaps because it was so serious that the teachers didn't feel able to bring him home and had had to enlist the help of his parents. We should also remember that foreign travel wasn't cheap in the 1960s and undoubtedly this had caused some discussion in Unitas Crescent. This must have happened when Smith was in his mid to late teens, and therefore some years before Margaret's murder.

This incident begins to open an informal window onto the issue of Smith's mental health and why he might have later been seen as 'disturbing' by Bob Beveridge and Ian Muir. Despite my best efforts, it is a window that I can barely open at all and I would have been loath to have even attempted to do so had not a couple of people told me that Smith had received treatment at Hartwood Hospital near Shotts. The informal window became a little more formal after it became more widely known what I was researching, and I started to look more closely at Hartwood Hospital.

Hartwood Hospital was originally opened in 1895 as the Lanark District Asylum and, with its sister hospital Hartwood Hill, which opened in 1935, it became the largest hospital complex in Scotland. By the 1950s it had grown to become one of the largest asylum developments in Europe, with over 2500 patients. At one stage it was completely self-sustaining and had its own farm, gardens, cemetery, railway line, staff accommodation, power plant and reservoir. It even trained its own nurses, as Margo proudly remembered: this was where she had trained, and she worked there for many years. Its original medical superintendent was Dr Archibald Campbell Clark, who stated that the goal of Hartwood Hospital was to 'cure where possible and give the best possible care when a cure cannot be found'. When he died, Clark was buried in the hospital cemetery. Hartwood aimed to create a community-like setting, with occupational therapies on offer; when something more was needed, it used electroconvulsive therapy (ECT), and it was the first place in Scotland to perform a lobotomy.

Hartwood Hospital closed in 1998 and much of the complex was destroyed by fire in 2004, although its imposing twin towers with their Scottish baronial detail survived and still dominate the North Lanarkshire landscape.

I do not know why, exactly when or how often John Smith was referred to Hartwood Hospital, but he was described to me as having been in an acute and locked ward, which suggests he had had an urgent and serious medical condition. I do not know the detail, because it is simply not possible to get copies of an individual's mental health records, as this would breach their medical confidentiality. I can therefore only speculate as to the nature of his illness, and do so with some experience of working with people who had acute and chronic mental health problems in my time managing the Acute Psychiatric Unit at HMP Grendon. My work there involved helping people with various forms of psychosis. These were men who had lost all insight that their disturbed thinking or emotion – which they believed to be normal and proper – was clearly inappropriate and that their bizarre behaviour was obvious to an outside observer. As such I regularly had to deal with people who were schizophrenic, had delusions, or were paranoid.

I wondered if Smith being hospitalised was why both Laura and Margo remembered hardly ever seeing him in the community. I wouldn't normally want to discuss the medical history of someone who is unknown to me, so as not to risk breaching their privacy, but it is important to do so in this case, as what I might discover and what I have already uncovered is germane to the issues which I have been describing. So too the incident on the school trip indicates some form of serious mental breakdown. It is hardly speculation to propose that Smith had little interest in socialising, or perhaps had gradually withdrawn from friends and even his family.

It struck me that these are two of the elements that regularly appear in the early onset of schizophrenia, which can come on in young men during puberty and in their teenage years. These elements are often accompanied with a drop in school performance, irritability and strange behaviour, and might later be accompanied by delusions, hallucinations and disorganised thinking. Many people with schizophrenia will see things or hear voices that don't exist and their speech will often include meaningless words that can't be understood. As a result, the schizophrenic will find it difficult to communicate and so will say very little, or their answers to questions put to them may be partially or completely unrelated.

We should remember here Bob and Ian's description of

the suspect that they encountered during their house-to-house enquiries and the fact that it hadn't taken them long to discover him. As we now know, this was undoubtedly John Smith. Was it simply the fact that they had been tasked with only a few houses to conduct their enquiries, or was there local intelligence to point them in this direction? I looked again at Bob's recollection of his interview with the man that they had encountered and re-examined what he remembered in the context of the symptoms of schizophrenia. Why were their interviewee's answers 'off the cuff'? Why did he not want to talk about the murder that had taken place only days before, and why did he start to tell them about stabbing cats? I also found myself returning once again to the comments Muncie made about the perpetrator and his appeal to the family of the killer to get him the attention that he might need.

Margaret had been overkilled, and a mountain of criminological research indicates that this is often indicative of the perpetrator having mental health issues. It is therefore very difficult not to read Muncie's comments without believing that he had been privy to local intelligence about the killer and specifically that the perpetrator needed 'attention'. What was being suggested was help with an underlying mental health problem. Muncie was also very publicly trying to be kind to the family of the perpetrator in appealing to them to come forward.

They did not.

Margo offered one final insight into Smith by describing her last encounter with him, although she couldn't be specific about the date. 'I remember seeing him when he as a bit older,' she said, 'at the top of Sandy Road. He had a hat on and he was smoking a pipe. He was not at all like the laddie that I remembered when I was a girl.'

Something had clearly happened to change his looks. Medication? Or perhaps simply the passing of time? At this point, I could only speculate.

I knew that I was going to have to try to track Smith down, but where should I start?

Was he even still alive?

*

I had repeatedly been told that John Smith had emigrated soon after the murder. If this was the case, how should we date Margo's final encounter with him in Sandy Road? And, more broadly, how soon was 'soon after the murder' and where had he gone to? As far as this last question was concerned, the consensus seems to have been Canada, so I decided to concentrate on this as my initial research focus.

How difficult could it be, I thought to myself, to track him down? After all, I had found Bob Beveridge within minutes. As it turned out, it was extremely difficult indeed.

Tapping in Smith's name or variations of it produced no positive results. Even using his middle name did not help. He had left no digital footprint and I began to wonder if perhaps, like Ian Muir, he had died before the onset of our technological age. Nor were there any positive results in the UK, although as he and his sister had attended Wishaw High School I was able to join a Facebook group of former pupils and was eventually able to locate his sister, who has since married and changed her name. She now lives in the east of Scotland. I sent her a friend request on Facebook, but she did not respond. Fair enough, I reasoned, as I too would be wary of accepting online requests from people I did not know. From what was publicly available on her Facebook page, she did not seem to have contact with her brother.

I also knew that if I had to use paper, as opposed to online, archives I would need a bit of luck to direct me to the right sources. Even so, if Smith had emigrated to Canada in 1973 (presuming that 'soon' would be in the weeks and months following the murder) he would have left a paper trail, and I had his full name and his date of birth to use as a starting point.

Still this was to be a frustrating process, because to access the relevant files held by the Canadian government I would have needed to be a Canadian citizen, or a family member of the person that I was trying to locate. Time to approach from a different angle. In the early 2000s I had spent several weeks conducting research in Toronto, and had made friends with a number of police officers who worked in the city. I called them up, explained my predicament and asked them if they had encountered anyone by that particular name, who might perhaps have committed offences – although I didn't think that this was likely. They hadn't, or on the few occasions when they had heard of someone by that name he was too young to have been the man who emigrated from Scotland in 1973.

My attempts to locate files on patients at Hartwood Hospital in the early 1970s were reaching a number of dead ends as well. I tried to think laterally. I was aware that Hartwood had been the setting for the formation of the Scottish Union of Mental Patients – which of course has the glorious acronym SUMP (a level below which it is impossible to sink) – by a group of patients in 1971. Laura and Margo had remembered that Smith had been 'clever' and a 'swot'. Perhaps he had also been involved with SUMP? I tracked down the twenty-seven signatories of their original manifesto, which was called 'Petition for the Redress of Grievances put forward by the patients in Hartwood Hospital, Shotts, Lanarkshire' and dated 18 August 1971. Though several of these signatories had been patients in the locked wards of the hospital, John Smith was not one of them.

I was rapidly realising that I needed a different strategy; one that would involve me getting specialist help.

*

I had been searching for an offender, an ex-offender and/or a mental health patient from the 1970s, who was believed to have emigrated to Canada and, frankly, I had discovered very little. This was in itself interesting, but hardly pushed forward my research. It was time to change tack and, instead of think-ing about Smith in any of the ways I had been employing, what if instead I considered him to be a missing person? There's a very different skillset needed in tracing missing people – especially someone who had gone missing in Canada – and so I started to look for investigators who had a background in geo-profiling, cold cases and expertise in internet searching, which are the components needed for this sort of task. If the investigator had also found missing people in the past, so much the better.

It turned out there was someone right in front of me. I had been following Doug MacGregor on Twitter for a few months, and had been impressed by what he had to say about personal safety, serious crime, policing and criminology more gener-ally, and his unique take on missing-persons cases. I soon discovered that he had his own company, based in Ottawa, and so asked him if he could send me his CV.

It arrived by email the next day.

I was most interested in the fact that Doug had taken courses in geo-profiling, crime mapping and advanced internet investigations at the British Columbia Institute of Technology, as I felt that these would be especially helpful in trying to locate Smith. Doug had also helped on police investigations in the USA related to suspicious deaths, cold cases and serial crimes involving murder, threats of violence and vandalism. He seemed like the ideal person to assist me in finding Smith and when I reached out about the case he readily agreed to help.

I had already sent off for a copy of Smith's birth certificate, as anyone is entitled to do in exchange for a small fee, and so could provide Doug with some basic information, plus I knew roughly when he might have moved to Canada. With Doug on the case, I felt certain that there would soon be a breakthrough.

That's not what happened.

I discovered that this sort of task takes time, and that you have to be patient and persistent if you are going to get results. In the meantime, Doug would send me regular email updates about what he'd been doing and what he had discovered, or not discovered as the case might be.

Unsurprisingly, Doug started by making enquiries at Immigration, Refugees and Citizenship Canada but was unable to obtain anything useful because of legal constraints – even Canadian citizens have limitations in what they are able to gain access to. He checked arrest, marriage and death notices in Canada after 1973, but again drew a blank. He had the same result when searching all the printed city telephone directories for major and mid-sized cities between 1973 and the present at the Library and Archives of Canada in Ottawa. He focused initially on cities that had international airports or ports, but he still could find nothing. In other words, there was no one with the right name and of a relevant age listed in the phone book. However, through these searches Doug did discover members of his extended family living in Ontario, and also several former classmates from Wishaw High now living in Canada.

These latter two results were interesting. After all, if Doug could discover his classmates, why could he not find out anything related to Smith? If he could discover relations of Smith, why could he find no mention of the man himself? This seemed to resonate with my own frustrations in trying to locate him in the UK; he did not seem to have made a footprint on either side of the Atlantic. To all intents and purposes he was invisible. There are echoes in all of this of how he was rarely seen in Unitas Crescent. I was beginning to think that Smith had probably died, but if he had this would surely have come up in Doug's search of death notices. I was torn as to what to conclude.

Just to be certain, Doug also looked at online records for Australia, New Zealand, South Africa and the USA. He also completed a social media search in all of these places too, but again he had no joy, although once more he found some members of his extended family living in these countries.

The most obvious conclusion was that Smith had never gone to Canada in 1973. Perhaps he simply went on holiday there? His extended family in Canada would have been able to facilitate a vacation – although even this would have shown up in the online search. I was beginning to form the impression that, if Smith was still alive, 'he's emigrated to Canada' had simply been a convenient fiction to spread about the town to cover for his sudden disappearance. If that was the case, we needed to ask *why* he had needed to disappear. Instead of looking further in Canada, I felt that I should simply return to the search for documents related to former patients at Hartwood Hospital, despite how unsuccessful my previous attempts had been.

Once again Doug's help proved invaluable when I felt that I had reached another dead end in my research.

Doug knew that I was beginning to despair a little but, through his mapping out of Smith's close and extended family's social media and online records, he was able to locate Smith's parents, who were in a nursing home close to where their daughter lived. However, there was still no mention of Smith, and Doug suggested that he should try a search of ScotlandsPeople. This is the official government site for the records of the Scottish state and the national archives. It was formed in 2011 following a merger between the General Register Office for Scotland and the National Archives of Scotland, and is usually the first port of call for people searching for their family's history. It houses statutory registers of births, marriages, deaths and so forth, as well as census returns and legal records from Scottish courts. I had consulted ScotlandsPeople early on in my research, but had drawn a blank.

Doug wanted to give it another go.

Through information gathered on the site and then once

more through using his mapping and social media expertise, he was eventually able to uncover a 'John Smith' close
to where his sister and his parents now lived and who was
roughly in the right age range.

I didn't have high hopes, and thought that this was just a
coincidence. It seemed rather far-fetched to imagine that this
could be the same John Smith who had once lived in Carluke,
especially given the persistent rumours in the town. However,
with the information that Doug provided I located an address
for this man but discovered that his telephone number was
ex-directory, blocking my plan to call him. That left writing
a letter. But what should that letter say? How honest should I
be about my research and why I might want to uncover where
Smith might now be living? I had reached my most serious
ethical dilemma – a dilemma that could only get more difficult if this was indeed the 'right' John Smith. Given that I
didn't know who this man might actually be, I wrote explaining that I was conducting research for a book about Carluke in
the 1970s, and 'I wonder if you might be the John Smith who
had once lived at 80 Unitas Crescent'. I said that if he was, I
would be interested in finding out what he might have done
by way of employment after leaving school.

I didn't mention the murder, and while I wrote to him as
'Professor David Wilson', I did not state directly that I was a
professor of criminology. I reasoned that if this wasn't the John
Smith I was searching for, then there was no need for this to
be of concern. If it was the man I was looking for, and he had
nothing to hide, then there was no harm in asking if he'd be
willing to answer some questions. I was just trying to establish
if he was in fact the man I had been searching for, and who most

people in Carluke believed had emigrated to Canada. Nor was I electronically invisible. If he had wanted to discover my academic background I have a website, am active on social media, have often been on TV and radio and am regularly quoted in the press. In other words, I have both electronic and traditional media footprints that he could easily have followed.

By this stage of my research I had actually resigned myself to the fact that the John Smith who had once lived at 80 Unitas Crescent, reportedly dated Margaret McLaughlin and who had undoubtedly been interviewed by Bob Beveridge and Ian Muir was dead. But still, I enclosed a stamped addressed envelope with my letter and waited for a reply.

A couple of weeks later an envelope landed on my hall floor at home and I immediately recognised the handwriting. It was my own. I could hardly contain myself. Were my hopes going to be dashed, or was I facing even more ethical dilemmas? The letter within the envelope was typed, and this is what it said:

I refer to your recent communication in which you invited me to participate in your research for your current project involving a book about Carluke in the 1970s. I do not believe I would have anything constructive to say about that time and therefore will respectfully decline to be involved in this matter. I wish you every success in your ongoing endeavours.

It was signed in ink with the name of the man that I had been searching for.

I'd found him.

*

The letter left me with a number of ethical dilemmas about how I should react to it, or indeed whether I *could* react. I could no longer continue my research in the belief that he was dead and, given that he was very much still alive, there were issues that I had to think through very carefully.

This letter had not just made Smith visible, but had also changed the dynamics about how I should conduct my research and the ethical basis on which I should operate – if that was even possible.

I needed to look more closely at the ethics and morality of what I was doing. These two things are closely related, but where ethics relates to right and wrong, and specifically how people should behave in different situations, morality is the personal conviction that an individual holds about particular behaviours. Ethics – and applying them so that we make an 'ethical' choice or decision – might involve putting these personal convictions to one side, because an ethical stance transcends the personal and involves more general rules.

As I am a member of the British Society of Criminology (BSC), an emeritus professor of criminology and a National Teaching Fellow, their ethical guidance was therefore my first port of call about whether I could continue and, if that was possible, exactly *how* I might proceed with my research. After all, I am writing about a murder, a miscarriage of justice and, as I see things, the wider failings of the Scottish criminal justice system; this is clearly the territory of criminology. I also consulted the National Union of Journalists' Code of Conduct, as I wanted to guide my behaviour in the most appropriate way. I would now have to deal with questions related to informed consent; the need to avoid causing harm or distress to research participants – especially those who might be vulnerable in some way; the public interest, and the wider issue of the public good.

The BSC's Statement of Ethics for Researchers in the Field of Criminology does not impose a single model of ethical practice on a criminologist, but simply provides a 'frame of reference'. This is intended to 'encourage and support reflective and responsible ethical practice in criminological research'. The top priority is to 'advance knowledge about criminological issues', in order that 'the maximum possible knowledge and benefits accrue to society'. These are laudable aims. The BSC wants free and independent inquiry about criminological matters and 'unrestricted dissemination of criminological knowledge'.

So far, so good.

However, they also state the need to minimise harm to research participants by ensuring that 'physical [and] psychological discomfort or stress' is minimised through ensuring the participants' informed consent. In other words, the research participant fully understands what it is that you are researching and is aware of the possible consequences of engaging with that research. Would Smith want to speak to me further (and let's leave to one side for the moment that he had written to me expressly stating that he did not) if he knew that I was not just researching more broadly about Carluke in the 1970s, but more specifically about the murder of Margaret McLaughlin and his possible role in that murder?

The BSC's guidance here is helpful, for they recognise that there are situations when harm, discomfort and stress are inevitable, especially when criminologists are researching issues related to 'uncovering corruption, violence or pollution'. Obviously violence and corruption are the context for understanding this case, specifically in relation to Margaret's murder, and then the more general matters that resulted in George Beattie being wrongly convicted.

This general permissiveness also applies to covert research. This is allowed 'when the ends might be thought to justify the means'. Some of the best research in criminology has been carried out covertly, such as that by Professor Nigel Fielding on the National Front, Professor James Treadwell about football hooligans in Birmingham and Sheffield, and Professor Simon Winlow on bouncers and the use of violence in the night-time economy.

As all of this indicates that 'there might be some circumstances where attempts to gain individual consent [from research participants] would be counterproductive'.

We need to think about what these circumstances might be and in what ways asking for consent might be counterproductive. This is when we need to consider what is deemed to be in the public interest. This is difficult to define, but is absolutely not just what the public might be interested in – the public interest here has a much broader meaning. At its simplest, the public interest is concerned with what is best for society as a whole and asks us all to act, or behave, in order to maintain or contribute to the public good. To act in the public interest is to also make life better for everyone. Defined in this way, acting in the public interest is to seek to right wrongs; uncover and then expose corruption; and to suggest better ways for individuals and institutions to act so that people are treated fairly, irrespective of race, class or gender.

I strongly believe that my research and investigation about this case contributes to the public good. It is always in the public interest to understand how a miscarriage of justice took place, so that such miscarriages might be avoided in future. Punishing the innocent and allowing the guilty to go free is in no one's interest; it does not contribute to the public good. Specifically, the search for justice in relation to Margaret's murder and who might really have been responsible is vital. More broadly, it is important to question why the Scottish criminal justice system closed its eyes and its ears to a flawed and frankly fraudulent police investigation and then repeatedly denied George Beattie justice. By doing so it is still – even now – denying him, and therefore also Margaret, justice.

It is important and a public good to have communities act together to hold individuals and institutions to account, especially those which are supposed to serve the public – as the criminal justice system must. All of us want to live in a society where there is a functioning and accountable criminal justice system, where crime is tackled and offenders punished and then rehabilitated; we need laws, courts, judges, lawyers, and probation, police and prison officers to make that criminal justice system work; and we need such a system to admit when it gets things wrong.

It is important to consider all of these factors. Smith may not want to be a participant in my research, indeed he has made it clear that he does not want to be, but should things be allowed to just be left to lie there? Why, as his letter states, does he not believe that he would have 'anything constructive to say' about that time? I understand that reluctance, especially if he felt that he was escaping local gossip, but why not simply state that? Even if it is only to share this with me and to tell me that he was wrongly suspected of having been involved in Margaret's murder, and so has had to move away to avoid the pressure of local chatter, that would still be hugely constructive. Was that why he became invisible? Looking at his wording it struck me that 'constructive' is an adjective, and its common meaning is to have a useful or beneficial purpose. But beneficial and useful *to whom*? It might not be constructive for Smith to say anything that might potentially harm him, but what if it is beneficial to George Beattie, Margaret McLaughlin and the Scottish criminal justice system?

There are other questions too. It's important to know if Smith remembers being interviewed by Ian Muir and Bob Beveridge, and what he said to them at the time. Above all, the case remains open in my mind as long as that strange claim that he 'might' have murdered Margaret remains unexplored.

The impression that I had from Smith's letter was that he sees himself as a victim; as someone who was damaged by what happened to Margaret, then by George's wrongful conviction and the rumours that were circulating in the town. He's the innocent party who was wrongly, if informally, accused through the gossip that was spreading at the time, but was never formally charged with anything untoward. Indeed, he was never even officially interviewed by the police. But if that's the case – and I really do accept that this might be a perfectly legitimate and accurate summary – why not seek out the opportunity to explain his version of events? He can hardly harm Margaret any further by doing so, and as far as the criminal justice system is concerned George is still the guilty party. Why not just use the occasion that has presented itself after all these years and get his story out into the public domain? Why not say, if it is indeed the case, 'I had some mental health problems which were made worse by local gossip and so I felt that I should move somewhere else'? Does he feel that he was driven away from Carluke and so has to remain in hiding?

I had various suspicions about why he might not want to get his story more publicly known but, no matter what, it seems to me that over the years Smith has been very able at avoiding answering these legitimate questions and so has benefited from what now appears to have been his silence, then his invisibility, George Beattie's wrongful conviction and repeatedly – if respectfully – declining to be 'involved in this matter'. After all, he didn't want to say anything to Ian Muir or Bob Beveridge nearly fifty years ago either. But, whether he likes it or not, Smith is involved in this matter for the simple reason that his name is constantly being brought up when the murder is discussed. The case continues to generate interest, controversy and debate, and Smith – fairly or unfairly – is part of that narrative.

From his letter I get the impression that he knew exactly what it was that I wanted to discuss with him. I wonder how he reacted when he received my letter. Perhaps he thought that after all of this time history had forgotten about him and the part he might have played in Margaret's murder, or that the rumours in the town had similarly long since dissipated. Smith must have known all about those rumours; that's why, I imagine, the fiction that he'd emigrated to Canada had been circulated and why he has no electronic footprint. But Smith wasn't stupid then, and nor is he stupid now. The language of his letter is formal and educated.

In truth, I wonder why he replied at all. He could have

remained invisible and unseen by choosing not to write back to me. It seems illogical to emerge after all this time. Indeed, if he hadn't replied I would have presumed he was dead and this would have gone no further. I feel like I'm walking in Bob Beveridge and Ian Muir's shoes once again. Smith is happy to accompany me to the police station to help with my enquiries, as long as we are actually only going to play cards and dominoes. It's a pleasant enough way to pass the time. He didn't put up much opposition to going to the police station in 1973 and he doesn't seem able to resist that same temptation now, albeit in the form of a letter.

I had a sneaking suspicion that he might really want to talk. Though perhaps he'd just heard about my research from someone in Carluke – after all, I've intentionally been open about it – and he knew that I would eventually want to speak to him. His letter was just a shot across my bows. Nonetheless, he reminds me of the young boys smoking in Carluke, cupping their cigarettes in their hands, wanting to be seen but unseen at the same time. 'He lifted up his jumper to show us the wounds to his abdomen.'

I could put my questions to him in another letter and wait and see if he would reply, but that didn't seem very likely. I doubt if writing again would push the research forward.

No, another journey needed to be made at this juncture; one that was practical, rather than philosophical.

However, before doing so I felt that I needed to set up an informal, academic sounding board to complement the Bake House Café. I didn't use this academic sounding board throughout my research, but only once I had tracked down Smith. Academics use peer review to validate their work and

I wanted to share my research with a few colleagues with relevant backgrounds and to gather their views about how I might progress it further. I asked three associates – a forensic psychologist and two senior criminologists – to consider what I had been doing and work with me on the issues that were emerging from what I had discovered. All three members of my academic sounding board had worked with violent offenders, had conducted research and written about violence, and still regularly work with the police.

They unanimously agreed that it would be best to try to meet Smith. I also felt that I needed to look him in the eye and ask my questions of him, in the full knowledge of what I have been able to uncover so far. He might have perfectly good answers to all of my questions, and so put to rest the rumour and innuendo that has survived for over four decades. He could state simply and directly that he had nothing to do with Margaret's murder. And, having been overt about every aspect of my research so far, I wanted to maintain that principle of openness. I want to knock on his door, introduce myself and explain what it was that I had been researching and why.

He might slam the door in my face. He would have every right to do so.

But perhaps, just perhaps, he might also avail himself of the opportunity to, for the first time, address himself to what he remembers of the night of Friday 6 July 1973, when Margaret McLaughlin was murdered after she had walked past 80 Unitas Crescent and used the shortcut into Colonel's Glen to catch the train into Glasgow.

No, best not write another letter. It was time to go and visit John Smith.

CHAPTER TEN

Meeting 'John Smith'

'I don't know what happened'

As I began my drive up the east coast of Scotland, I had a lot to think about, and a great deal of work ahead of me. Quite apart from fitting in a talk for my sister Annie in Fife, I was toying with the idea of dropping in on Bob Beveridge in Falkland. At the very least, I thought that it would be lovely to visit his violin shop. Perhaps he'd let me take him out for a coffee and I could bring him up to speed with my research. I then started to worry that I was making a classic tourist error in imagining that every town is like Brigadoon and underestimating the distance between them. I remember laughing at a TV producer in 2010 who thought that I could 'just pop over the border' from Glasgow, where I had been lecturing, to Rothbury in Northumberland, where the murderer Raoul Moat was hiding out. 'They're actually not that close,' I pointed out, and added, 'It will take me hours to get there and I will arrive after the midday news.' That was the deal-breaker, as far as that request was concerned.

However, this time there was more than geography on my mind.

A conversation with the forensic psychologist on my academic sounding board was still ringing in my ears. The Saturday before my trip north had been dominated by my discussions with him about the Carluke case. I'd brought him up to speed with all my research. One aspect that I really wanted his view on was why Smith had replied to my letter. Later I wrote up our conversation; his insight was illuminating.

His first thought was that Smith's family could have replied on his behalf. A possibility, sure enough, but I asked him to assume that the reply had come from Smith himself, and speculate why he might do so. He pointed out that it is not unusual for people who have committed serious offences to feel the need to talk about them, as if they need to let it all out. He went on to say that this is particularly so if the perpetrator is insane.

The forensic psychologist's use of the adjective 'insane' wasn't meant to be cruel, flippant or a cheap shot – yet nor was it a clinical diagnosis. Insane is a legal term rather than a medical one and is related to a defendant's ability to determine right from wrong. The word itself comes from Latin – *sanus* means healthy. The forensic psychologist was using this description to indicate a spectrum of behaviours that we had discussed, and which he felt were characterised by abnormal mental or behavioural patterns. These abnormal mental or behavioural patterns do not necessarily mean that the person is unaware of what they have done, or that what they did was wrong.

Nonetheless, the word pulled me up short.

I wondered if we can still credibly call someone 'insane', especially as that description has seeped into general usage. It's the same with 'crazy'. What these words seem to imply now is something – particularly an experience – that is especially different, pleasurable and unique, and therefore something aspirational and to be savoured, as opposed to the original meaning as an oppressive and negative way of labelling people. I was reminded of the sign at 30 Glenburn Terrace, saying '30, Nut House', and of Bob Beveridge's description of the man that he and Ian Muir had interviewed as 'a bit of a nutter'.

I asked the forensic psychologist to sketch out his worries more generally about my journey up from England to meet with Smith. He wondered if it was ethical, and so I described to him the various principles outlined by the BSC, and although in the end he agreed that it was ethical he also suggested that I could perhaps just let readers come to their own conclusions about Smith without the trip. However, I felt that not going to see him and at the very least trying to speak with him would be letting people in Carluke down; it would be a loose end that I couldn't leave untied. By extension I would be letting readers and everyone else down as well.

We talked about how Smith might react to my knocking on his door. I had worked with another member of the academic sounding board in an applied setting, where we have had to manage offenders with underlying mental health problems, and none of us were naive about the difficulties that I might encounter. Even so, it is worth re-stating once again that most people who are mentally ill are not dangerous, and are more at risk of being attacked, or of harming themselves rather than other people.

Nonetheless, as journalists and investigative reporters know only too well, every 'doorstep' has its risks and I did not want to underestimate how careful I would have to be. I believed that the risks could be managed. I took precautions by explaining what I was doing to a handful of colleagues, including the forensic psychologist on the academic sounding board, sharing with them Smith's address and, with one of the two criminologists on the academic sounding board, the time that I would be knocking on his door. If I had not made contact with this colleague within thirty minutes of that time, they were to phone the police.

Having been in enough of these situations, I am usually a good judge of them and didn't think that that would be necessary.

Fingers crossed.

*

It seemed appropriate that I was listening to Rachel Podger as I drove into Falkland; after all, I was visiting a violin shop. I'd decided that I would drop in on Bob and had phoned ahead to make arrangements to meet up with him at his shop. It was early, so early he hadn't opened when I reached Falkland, and so I took the opportunity to grab a coffee at a café across the road from his shop, which also doubled as a gift shop selling jewellery and Scottish souvenirs. I could have used that same description for almost all the shops up and down the length of Falkland's main street.

I took a chair at the window with my flat white.

Almost immediately a large, sleek bus pulled up and disgorged a gaggle of tourists. They were loud and excited. It was soon clear from their accents that they were Americans.

I knew that Falkland Palace – which still dominates the town, and is where Mary, Queen of Scots once played tennis – was a tourist attraction, but I was still bemused by the numbers that seemed to be getting off the bus.

Laura, who had made my flat white, came over and looked out of the window. That gave me an opportunity to ask about some local history and specifically why there was an American fascination with Falkland.

She smiled at my question and said, 'It's mostly a female thing! Falkland is the setting for *Outlander*. Have you seen it?'

I shook my head and Laura explained about the *Outlander* books and TV series, which has been described in some reviews as '*Downton Abbey* for the Highlands'. In other words it's a tartan fantasy – the lid of a Christmas biscuit tin come to life. Despite the critical reaction, it is very popular and that popularity has helped to transform Falkland's economy.

As if proving the point, Laura introduced me to her friend Rebecca, who had just popped into the shop and proceeded to explain that she made jewellery specifically to sell to tourists. One of her most popular lines was a silver bracelet on which was engraved a line from the wedding vows of the protagonists in *Outlander*: 'Blood of my blood, and bone of my bone. I give you my body that we two may be one.'

Rebecca joked that when she's working on these bracelets she says the oath in a broad – and fake – Scottish accent. You know, the sort of accent that people put on when they're trying to impersonate what a Scottish accent sounds like and which, in turn, seems to have become accepted as 'Scottish'. I asked if Rebecca would recite the vows in her fake accent for me and she did indeed sound like a female version of Groundskeeper

Willie from *The Simpsons*. All three of us laughed and I marvelled at the fact that a series of romantic and fantasy novels by an American author about the Jacobite uprisings was being consumed as an authentic insight into Scotland and Scottish history. It is easy to sneer, but I had every reason to be grateful – not least being able to drink a flat white at that time in the morning. It didn't take too long for me to reflect on the differences with Carluke's High Street; I certainly didn't see a food bank, or any charity or betting shops.

Laura, Rebecca and I moved on to discuss whether this tourism was a good or a bad thing as it destroyed, or perhaps more charitably transformed, those things that were authentic to Falkland and to Scottish history. Before we could come to any sort of conclusion I noticed that Bob had opened his shop and so I made my excuses, finished my coffee and crossed the road.

Bob met me at the door of his shop and shook my hand; it was hard not to notice that he had a firm grip. He was in his late seventies, at least six feet tall, thin, and appeared to be very fit. He told me that he walked every day and had only recently given up running, after having fallen out of bed.

He ushered me inside.

The shop is an Aladdin's cave filled not just with violins, violas and cellos, but also with antiques, books, paintings and ceramics. These goods all seem to be in a jumble, with no obvious order as to how they are displayed. In fact, they were arranged so precariously here and there, dotted about the shop and in every available space, that I had to be very conscious of where I was walking as we went through to a back room.

I sat down, relieved that I hadn't knocked anything over. I thanked Bob for all of his help and brought him up to speed with what I had discovered. I also said that I had a few remaining questions that I wondered if he might be willing to answer. Like a good, no-nonsense Scot, he readily agreed. Specifically, I asked, whether the suspect that he and Muir had encountered had been alone when they had knocked on his door, or if he was with other members of his family. The question was prompted by my still being curious about Muncie's comment to the press about the family of the culprit coming forward. Bob couldn't remember, although he was able to add a number of elements to the story he had previously told me, and provide a little more detail. The following is an extract of our conversation:

DW: Did you actually arrest your suspect?

BB: Well, he was deprived of his liberty but he didn't make any protest about us taking him to the station. In those days no one questioned the police.

DW: What do you remember about the wounds to his torso?

BB: They weren't serious and he certainly didn't need hospital treatment. They might have been self-inflicted, or they could have been a result of a struggle. You know, he was a bit of a nutter – totally unconcerned that he was in a serious situation, as we were talking to him about a murder.

DW: And you did discuss the murder?

BB: Yes, but that was also what was strange. He never really said anything – even how

horrible a case it was. As I wrote to you, he
also mentioned stabbing cats to justify the
wounds on his abdomen. Looking back, it was
almost as if he wanted to be seen as the victim.
He was the strangest person that I have ever
interviewed because his attitude was calm and his
explanations so very disturbing.

During our conversation Bob also suggested to me that there
had been jealousy within the investigation about the fact that
the Scottish Crime Squad had become involved. 'We were never
welcomed' was how he characterised this, and he felt that had
played a role in subsequent developments. Specifically, both he
and Ian Muir weren't too surprised when 'their' suspect was let
go and George Beattie, who was being interviewed by the local
and regional police, was charged. In other words, the investigation had become a professional turf war, with Lanarkshire
detectives, the 'Masonic Lodge with truncheons', determined to
prove their competency by being the first to charge a suspect –
even if that meant charging the wrong one.

I was aware from the noise outside that another tour bus
had pulled up and that Bob was getting anxious to serve the
people who were coming into his shop. We carefully returned
to the front of the shop. I took my leave of him as he sold two
ancient-looking books to a young woman from Arizona.

Sadly we never did find time to have a coffee.

I had to move on and drive further north.

*

John Smith's flat was a thirty-minute walk from the hotel I had
booked. I'd asked for directions and could tell by the look on

the receptionist's face that she was confused as to why I would want to go there. I didn't feel able to explain, and so I just left her looking bemused as I set off into the day.

Directions in hand, I marched purposefully outside of the hotel and pulled the hood of my jacket over my head, as a token gesture against the rain.

The walk took me out of the town centre into a liminal area that wasn't quite in the country, but nor was it truly rural. I used the walk as an opportunity to go over the questions that I wanted to ask and, perhaps more importantly, the phrases that I would use if it became obvious that Smith was going to slam the door in my face. 'I've come a long way,' I would say, and 'can you not just give me five minutes of your time?'

The walk also allowed me to think about the order of the questions and I ran over that order several times in my head, so as to get the structure completely clear. After all, I couldn't just blurt out the questions which were the most crucial for the research, but had to carefully lead up to them. I had to get Smith into a safe psychological and interpersonal space where he felt able to answer my questions. Knowing the structure of my questions would also allow me to concentrate on the answers that he might be willing to give.

The receptionist was correct. After half an hour I located the street where Smith lived and then the block of flats to which I had sent my letter months ago.

I walked past the block to gather my thoughts and then looked back to see if I could spot anything obvious. I'm not exactly certain what it was that I was expecting to see. I then called my friend to put in place our agreed safety arrangements. From a security perspective I knew that the best scenario for me was to engage Smith in conversation on his doorstep and the worst would be to be invited into his flat. Being inside his own home would give Smith a measure of power and control, whereas if I was still at the front door I could make a quick exit should the need arise. I didn't think that would be necessary, especially as I really was expecting him to tell me to get lost – or more colourful words to that effect.

If I am honest, as I stood looking at the apartment complex I was excited rather than scared and I put my quickening heartbeat down to anticipation rather than fear. This was the culmination of all my months of research so far. Answers – to confirm or deny my hypothesis, for better or worse – were behind that door.

After a few moments I walked back to the flats, scanned the various buzzers and found the one belonging to Smith.

I took a deep breath; it had all come down to this. Months of research immersed in a variety of libraries and on different websites; Bake House Café sounding boards and walks up and down Carluke's impoverished High Street; my criminological autopsy in Colonel's Glen and Unitas Crescent; fake trails in Canada; and now here I was, standing with my finger poised to ring the doorbell of my prime suspect.

I pushed the buzzer. It didn't seem to make a noise; I pushed a little harder the second time and then waited. Still no response, and so I tried a third time.

All I heard was silence.

Smith was not at home.

I noticed a service buzzer and pushed that. As I did so the front door of the building opened and I stepped inside. The lobby was cold and unlit but I was still able to locate Smith's flat, which was on the ground floor to my left. I knocked on the door, but it was clear that no one was inside. I knocked on his neighbour's door, but got no reply there either. I stood for a few moments, somewhat lost and thinking about what I should do. I looked in my rucksack and found some paper; I decided to write Smith a note using the same phrases that I had mentally rehearsed. I also told him where I was staying and invited him to come for a cup of tea that evening at six o'clock.

I pushed my missive through his letterbox knowing as I did so that Smith would never turn up at my hotel and that he had no intention of ever having a cup of tea with me. That's not the kind of person he had ever been. I remembered that Laura and Margo had described him as not really having a social group when they were growing up. It all felt like a wasted journey. What had I been expecting? Most investigations end up like this – inconclusive and unsatisfying, with questions left unanswered or, in my case, not even asked. This was real life and not a 9 p.m. crime drama, where everything is neatly packaged up in under an hour, ready for the next episode.

Perhaps my note might encourage him to write to me again, but that didn't seem too likely either.

I felt deflated.

But then everything changed. Of course, I can't give a detailed account of what happened next, for legal reasons, but I can distil what I found out about John Smith in the next few minutes. I learnt that he lives alone and has barely any contact with his neighbours. He doesn't have a car, and doesn't drive. I also realised that I had never seen a photograph of Smith before, so I didn't know what he looked like.

I was about to head back to the hotel when I decided to have one last look around the side of the building, just in case Smith's bedroom curtains were drawn. Perhaps he was asleep – though it was a bit late to still be in bed.

I edged around a tiny scrub of garden to look at Smith's bedroom window. The curtains were open and I had to face reality – he was not at home.

I returned to the front of the apartment block and, with some sense of shame, peered through Smith's front window. I quickly scanned what I could see. I noticed some 'Happy 70th Birthday' cards on the mantelpiece, even though his seventieth birthday had been several months before. There were framed photographs of his family on otherwise bare walls. There was a sofa, and a coffee table that held a copy of Lynda La Plante's *Hidden Killers*. My guilt overcame me and I looked away.

*

I sat drinking tea in the hotel and tried to work out what I could do, feeling I was left with few options. Should I just let the Bake House Café come to their own judgement, based on what I had discovered so far, or instead wait around a little longer to see if Smith might return home?

But what if he had gone on holiday and wouldn't return for a week or so?

Weighing everything up, I knew that I would have to go back, even if that meant returning to his empty flat and peering through his window once more. I finished my tea under the watchful eye of the receptionist and headed back out, into the rain.

On my return journey I walked with a little more certainty,

shaving five minutes off the time now that I knew the way. Again I walked past the specific address and then looked back towards Smith's front window. There were no lights on but I noticed that my note was lying on the coffee table. He must have seen it, but had he gone out again? I peered a little more closely and then realised that he was sitting on his sofa reading a newspaper; I could see it was a broadsheet, though I couldn't make out which one. I marched to the door and rang the bell.

I couldn't hear anything and I thought that perhaps it wasn't working, or that he had had the bell disengaged. I realised that there was only one thing for it – I went to the front of his flat, knocked on his window and waved.

I wasn't going to be ignored.

Smith seemed displeased and very grumpy as he looked up and then out at me, and I didn't really blame him. He slowly put his newspaper down on the coffee table and shakily got up from his sofa. His hair was white with age, and he had been using a pair of glasses to read his newspaper. He was above average height and overweight, and I watched him slowly shuffle, rather than walk, from his sofa towards the door. He could easily have been mistaken for a man in his mid to late eighties.

I moved away from the window, but in my excitement I forgot to call my friend about our security arrangements, and nor did I turn on my phone to record the ensuing conversation. The door opened, and for the first time I was able to see Smith face to face. A scar on the right-hand side of his face bisected his lips; he had blue eyes, but what was most striking of all was his pure snow-coloured hair. He had perched his reading glasses on his head.

I wasn't invited inside.

Below is a transcript of our conversation. I have taken out the 'ums' and 'erms' but have left in obvious pauses and also added in some minor editorial detail, such as when Smith smiled, or when his voice rose and the sometimes curious noise that he made when he spoke, almost as if his teeth didn't fit properly. I hurriedly wrote down the transcript as soon as our conversation had finished but the fixed order of my memorised questions provided me with a structure to remember what we had discussed. In total we spoke for only about ten minutes.

DW: Mr Smith?

JS: That's right.

DW: I've come a long way to talk to you.

JS: No. No. My sister and my brother-in-law wrote to you. I don't want to talk to you. These things are in my past and I'm not well. I can't help you.

DW: I'm sorry, have you not been well?

JS: I'm no [*sic*] going into that; that's my business. I wish you well with your book, but I can't help you at all.

DW: I was writing about Carluke in the 1970s and especially about what happened to Margaret McLaughlin.

JS: Yes, a sad case.

DW: So, that's what I was interested in talking to you about. What are your memories of the murder?

JS: Well I'm no [*sic*] getting involved in that.

DW: OK. I understand. I did get the letter. Thank you—

JS: Beattie murdered Margaret McLaughlin. That is

fact. I can tell you that is fact but I can't go into any details. [His voice rises] Beattie definitely murdered Margaret McLaughlin.

DW: OK. OK. [Trying to calm him down.] Well, thank you for that. I've been looking for you for quite a wee while. Everyone in Carluke thought that you had emigrated to Canada, so I have even been looking for you there! [I laugh]

JS: No, I didn't go to Canada. [He smiles]

DW: I just needed someone to talk about the murder, that was what I wanted to discuss, but I understand if you can't speak to me.

JS: I can't get into it but what happened was very, very sad and very, very bad. She didn't deserve that.

DW: You went out with her for a wee while, didn't you?

JS: No! [Voice rises again] I was a friend of hers; I didn't go out with her.

DW: You were just a friend?

JS: She lived around the corner. She had a boyfriend. [Pause] He—

DW: Bob?

JS: Yes. He went to South Africa and got a house there. It was Beattie. I can't tell you anything but her brothers Eddie and John [his teeth start to chatter] they definitely know that Beattie murdered Margaret McLaughlin. I can't talk about it. I'm not bringing it out. It's up to people in authority to bring it out. I'm just low down the scale. I'm just an Indian.

DW: I spoke with a number of your former neighbours

from Unitas Crescent. I was intrigued by their
description of you. 'You would have looked twice at
him; he was very handsome.'

JS: I don't know about that. [He smiles]

DW: That was how Laura and Margo remembered you –
as a handsome man. Margo was a runner.

JS: I've got a very bad memory, especially concerning
my past. I can't even have a conversation with you
about these people. I have no memory. I just have
to get on by myself now. Margaret McLaughlin was
definitely murdered by Beattie. That is a fact; that is
fact. A fact. [Voice rises as he says this]

DW: OK. I'm grateful that you came to the door.

JS: I can't go into detail about what I was doing, or
anything like that. I've just got myself now and
[names sister] and I'm taking it nice and easy. It's
coming up to fifty years!

DW: Did you work, Mr Smith? After Wishaw High
School, what work did you do?

JS: I'm no [*sic*] going into that [voice rises]. If you are
interested in Margaret McLaughlin I can say that
Beattie definitely murdered Margaret McLaughlin
and her brothers will confirm that. Beattie writes
incessantly – even now he says that he never
murdered Margaret McLaughlin. He's done his
time, why does he not just say that he did it?

DW: Perhaps because he didn't. There are people in the
town who think that you did.

JS: I don't know what happened. He definitely did it
[voice rises again]. They got the right man. I wish

you well with your book. As time goes on you will
realise why I can't talk to you.

DW: I think that I know a wee bit about what
happened to you.

JS: [Says something I could not make out]

DW: I know a wee bit about your time in Hartwood. Are
you not well at the moment?

JS: No, at the moment I am good.

DW: Good?

JS: My sister and my brother-in-law are there for me.
I'm just on my own in that wee house. I can't help
you. [Closes door]

As the door shut I ran around the corner, sat down on the
pavement and wrote up my notes. The rain from the pavement
seeped through my trousers but I barely noticed as I was
so intent on putting everything down on paper. I scribbled
away for about thirty minutes and then, when I had finished,
started my walk back to the hotel. Over the next few hours
I would pore over that conversation, trying to make sense of
what Smith had said or refused to discuss, and lamenting the
questions that I couldn't put to him because he'd closed the
door before I had been able to ask them.

*

The interview might have been brief but, allied with my most
recent conversation with Bob Beveridge, it felt remarkably
revealing. In particular I was struck by how this doorstep
conversation echoed a number of themes that had emerged
in 1973. The most obvious of these themes have to do with
memory and remembering; the sense that it was Smith who

was the victim, either because it was him who had been stabbed or, almost the first thing that he had said to me, that he was or had been unwell; and how evasive he had been about Margaret's murder, and indeed about himself.

Even so, Smith did provide new information. Specifically that he had never gone to Canada, despite all the persistent rumours in the town, and nor did he deny anything when I had mentioned his being in Hartwood Hospital.

Let's think a little more about these themes and what they might suggest. Does what he said shed more heat than light?

Smith states several times that he has no memory, or has such a bad memory that he can't even discuss people who had once been his neighbours, such as Laura or Margo, although he does remember the names of Margaret's brothers. However, there seems to be more going on here than simply forgetting, or not being able to remember. In the other phrase that crops up on several occasions – that he is 'no [*sic*] going into that', or getting 'into it' because it is 'his business' – Smith implies that he does remember but doesn't want to share the information. What is this 'it' or 'that' which he doesn't want to get into? Most immediately it would appear that 'it' is about the murder of Margaret, but would also include offering details about what work he might have done on leaving school and the cause of the poor state of his health. These latter issues seem like trivial details but Smith does not want to share them, or really explain why sharing them would be so problematic. Perhaps this is why he made no comment when I raised Hartwood Hospital. I was also left wondering if Smith's physical appearance – including the shuffling way that he walked and his weight – might have been down to medication that he was taking. The overall tone of his speech was also somewhat flat and, the couple of occasions when he got angry notwithstanding, the way he spoke was monotone and lifeless. This again might be down to medication.

His lack of memory and that he couldn't go into any details is very similar to what had happened when he had been interviewed by Beveridge and Muir in 1973. Bob remembered that 'he wasn't prepared to talk about the murder at all'. Despite that, on his doorstep Smith felt able to offer as 'fact' that Margaret had been murdered by George Beattie. He used the word 'fact' five times in our brief discussion and so it stands out, given the imprecision or avoidance about everything else that he said. Why was this a 'fact'? Was he meaning that it is a fact given that George has been convicted of the murder, or is he implying some other direct knowledge of the murder?

I was also intrigued by two other aspects of our conversation. First, the curious way that Smith always used Margaret's full name, distancing himself from her, even though he had been prepared to admit (on my prompting) that she had been 'a friend'. Secondly, I was struck by the idea that Smith was 'low down the scale' and therefore 'just an Indian' and that it was 'up to people in authority to bring it out'. Here's yet again another 'it' for us to consider, with all the implications that there is something that is not yet in the public domain, but which he is privy to. This also might simply be paranoia.

Smith stated that he was confused as to why George Beattie just doesn't admit to Margaret's murder, having served his sentence. He also uses the phrase 'writes incessantly' and I think that Smith meant George writing in, or to, newspapers. However, I have never encountered anything that George himself has written journalistically, so I am presuming that Smith meant the people who had campaigned on his behalf. I am certain that he didn't mean that George had written personally to him. After all, it had taken me months of research to find an address – research that I doubted George would have been able to undertake. When I pointed out that George's continued refusal to accept guilt for the murder might be a consequence of the fact that he hadn't actually killed Margaret and pressed the point that there were other people in the town who thought that Smith was the guilty party, he merely replied, 'I don't know what happened' and again blamed George Beattie.

How should we interpret that statement, 'I don't know what happened', coming as it does immediately after I had pointed out that many people believed that Smith might be the murderer? Is there yet another echo of his interview with Bob and Ian, when he had replied to their questions about whether he had killed Margaret? In 1973 he said, 'I might have. I don't remember what I did yesterday,' which seems to mirror his response to my statement that people thought that he might be the murderer.

The other recurrent theme is that Smith is unwell. In 1973 it was the superficial wounds to his torso and Bob's feeling that this was meant to convey that it was Smith, rather than Margaret, who was the victim. Now, at his doorstep, it was some unspecified physical or mental illness which had caused him to be unwell, although he also stated that he was not unwell at that moment in time. Again a portrayal of himself as a victim, rather than Margaret, and while he did accept that her murder was both bad and sad, the words and phrases that he used were without genuine emotion. He had 'flat affect', so that he did not seem to me to convey empathy about the fact that a friend of his had been brutally murdered. He knew the appropriate words, but he did not seem to me to understand their meaning, or the emotion that would commonly be associated with them.

No matter how I interpreted our brief exchange, I have to acknowledge that I found Smith deeply unknowable and, at times, incomprehensible. Ironically, while George Beattie inserted himself into the story of Margaret's murder and talked endlessly about it as a means to connect him to the investigation into her death, Smith seems intent on distancing himself from it. When he did at last speak about her murder, what he said was cryptic and open to interpretation. Smith gave me the impression that everything he said was carefully scripted. He presents a narrative that is linear and black and white, rather than the messy, grey chaos that characterises most of our lives. Scripts such as these are repetitive and seem to offer a 'truth', but they also fail to accommodate the gaps and the inconsistencies which emerge when that 'truth' is subjected to scrutiny.

For me, Smith seemed to be parroting words and phrases that he had heard, and thereafter used, many times before. I am not suggesting that he was consciously following a script, but it is hardly speculation to suggest that my letter must have generated some discussion about what had happened in Carluke in 1973. Perhaps phrases such as 'it's in my past', 'it's for people in authority to bring it out' and 'it has been nearly fifty years' were the cornerstones of that discussion.

Even the best cornerstones can, over time, become weak.

If, as Smith repeatedly stated, George Beattie's guilt is a

'fact', there really shouldn't be any problem with him discussing what he had done for work after leaving Wishaw High School. I accept that it is his 'business', but Margaret was his friend and so why would he not want to offer more help, even if she was murdered nearly half a century ago? There is no reason for that sort of detail to remain hidden. Might it be because the truth, or at least another version of the truth, emerges from the answers to this and other seemingly minor questions, and when put together create a very different narrative from the one that he wants to present? Truth, in my experience, is usually ugly and messy and not at all straightforward, which is of course why it makes such demands of us, given that we all strive to be beautiful, innocent and perfect.

However, no matter how ontologically complicated it becomes to determine the truth, or how unknowable Smith might seem, at the end of the day there is something which is known and which is true: Margaret McLaughlin was murdered. More than this, I would also say with absolute certainty that, after all the research I have undertaken, I am more, not less, convinced of George Beattie's innocence. For me, his guilt is most certainly not a 'fact' at all.

So who did murder Margaret McLaughlin?

*

That night I stayed in my hotel room thinking about what had happened during the day and read and re-read the transcript of the conversation with John Smith. Having been trained initially as an historian, I tend to become quite focused on documents and specifically what is being said and left unsaid, by whom and in what particular circumstances. How does all of this relate to other things that have been said at different times? What patterns emerge, and can these allow us to form a judgement about the issues that we are interested in resolving? Sometimes this focus can become obsessive, and that is unhelpful; there are times when you simply have to accept what is being said at face value – there is no deep or hidden meaning. As Freud is said to have joked, 'sometimes a cigar really is just a cigar'.

I want to heed that warning, while also drawing attention to a number of extraordinary answers that Smith gave in our exchange. The first is the reply that he offered to my observation that many people in the town thought that he had murdered Margaret. To this he immediately countered 'I don't know what happened', before again insisting that the murder had been committed by George. This answer is in itself obviously contradictory – he does not know what happened, but then states that George is guilty. Indeed, he repeatedly states that George was guilty; that this guilt was a 'fact'. However, his answer can be interpreted to suggest a lack of knowledge about the murder and the events surrounding the murder: 'I don't know what happened.'

There is, of course, another way to interpret that phrase. It can also be taken to mean 'I wasn't myself and I was acting out of the ordinary; I don't know what came over me.' These meanings hint at losing control and acting irrationally in the heat of the moment; they suggest being shocked and surprised by the consequence of losing control. This seems to chime with a comment that he had made to Bob and Ian in 1973, but to be certain this analysis needs to be pursued more formally and therefore not just by me.

The second answer relates to Smith being 'just an

Indian' – which I have taken to mean that therefore he wasn't a 'chief' – and that it was for 'people in authority to bring it out', as he was just 'low down the scale'. I am presuming that these comments relate to the murder and specifically that there is something that had been said privately by the police, but which hasn't yet emerged into public discourse. I had reflected on this at the start of my research and wondered if the police might have realised that they had got the wrong man when they charged George, but then found it all too complicated and embarrassing to back-track. The 'Masonic Lodge with truncheons' knew they had got it wrong, but to have admitted that would have had the Scottish Crime Squad laughing in their faces. That wouldn't have been an ideal situation if the senior investigating officer – 'Scotland's top detective' – was seeking promotion. So perhaps they had let it be known that they had some evidence that they couldn't discuss publicly but which proved George's guilt. They might also have done this as a way of assuaging any worries that Margaret's family might have had about George's conviction, because they would have been as aware as everyone else of what was being discussed in Unitas Crescent.

That thought had occurred to me after I received an email telling me that my correspondent knew George was guilty because his mother had handed his bloodstained overalls in to the police. That simply wasn't true, but how had the person who had emailed me begun to imagine this extraordinary scenario? It smacked of Hollywood, rather than Carluke! Even so, I wanted to check it out with the Bake House Café sounding board. I also wanted to know why Smith seemed so certain that Margaret's brothers knew the truth.

Finally, why did Smith think that 'as time goes on you will

realise why I can't talk to you'? What is he implying here? That he does know something about the murder that involves him keeping a secret, or is this just another aspect of his being an 'Indian', rather than a 'chief'? Perhaps it suggests that there might come a time when he will speak?

These answers were extraordinary, but how relevant were they and did they bring my investigation to a conclusion?

Gradually I grew sleepy and as I knew that the following afternoon I had an appointment at the Bake House Café I decided to go to bed. I had a long drive in front of me, but I was eager to share my discussions with Smith and to see what everyone made of his answers. It was because of my sisters and their friends that I had begun this journey and so it was important for me to end it back home in Carluke, where it had all started.

Would Smith's statements about George Beattie's guilt convince them, or would they still be as certain of his innocence as they had been back in 1973?

CHAPTER ELEVEN

Back in the Bake House Café

'It's up to people in authority to bring it out'

I had some unfinished business to attend to before I reported back to everyone in the Bake House Café. Given I had missed him the last time I was in Carluke, I wanted to meet up with Douglas Forrest, my friend from school who now works as a lawyer in the town. After my drive from the east coast of Scotland back to Carluke I once again walked up the High Street, but instead of making my way to the Bake House Café I soon found myself in Douglas's office, shaking his hand.

He gestured for me to take a seat and, after we had exchanged pleasantries, I apologised for my rushed visit the last time I had been in the town. I explained what I had been researching and outlined my discoveries in relation to Margaret's murder and George's conviction. He nodded sagely when I characterised George's conviction as a 'fit-up' by the police.

Douglas listened closely to everything I said, and afterwards surprised me by asking, 'Did you know I had been at primary school with George? He was in my class.' I didn't know this at all and queried, 'But surely you are too young?' Douglas explained that George had been kept back for a couple of years. George was, of course, physically much larger than the other pupils, but Douglas explained that this had never been a problem; he hadn't bullied the other children or pushed his weight around. The next question was the one I had really come to ask.

'So, did you think that he killed Margaret McLaughlin?'

'No,' he replied immediately, 'he just didn't have that sort of violence in him.'

I shared with Douglas that I had spoken with George's original solicitor and that he had said much the same thing. It is worth noting that lawyers are regularly in the company of people who have been accused of crimes that they did or did not commit and therefore usually develop an acute 'sixth sense' of who might be lying – or who might be telling the truth.

We chatted on for a further half-hour about the state of the High Street and how conveyancing is now his main business, given that so many people come into the town and then go again. I checked my watch, explained I had to get to the café and promised that we should catch up properly the next time I was back home.

What struck me more than anything else from this conversation, especially as it came so soon after my exchange with John Smith, was that those people who knew George were almost unanimous in their belief of his innocence, rather than trusting that his guilt was a fact.

Nor had Douglas been in the least surprised when I described George's conviction as a 'fit-up'.

I walked back from Douglas's office past the space where the post office had once stood, crossed the road and then made my way into Clyde Street and the Bake House Café.

*

By the time I got there Laura and Margo were already having a coffee, and Maureen arrived soon after I arrived. Laura told me how excited she was to hear what I had discovered. I hoped that I wouldn't disappoint her. I took a seat opposite Margo and, as I did so, Alison, Margaret and Willie came into the café.

As we all sat down, a couple also appeared and took seats by the window. Laura and Margo looked concerned but I told them, 'It's fine – this isn't a secret.'

I explained that I wanted to read some things to them, but, before that, I brought them up to speed with everything that had happened in the three months since we'd last been together. I was especially interested in their reaction to the email about George's bloodstained overalls. Maureen laughed, saying that Mrs Beattie had gone to her grave 'cursing Muncie – she would have done no such thing'. However, my sister Margaret said that she had a hazy memory of something like this being discussed at school, although she couldn't remember who had started the rumour and nor, when I pushed her, could she be certain about the details. Even so, she was adamant that no one had believed any of this to be true. To be absolutely clear, no bloodstained overalls have ever been produced and it was quickly established that George was wearing other clothing when he had gone off to work on the night of the murder. The story feels very much like nonsense to me. George may have worn overalls *at* his work – perhaps they were kept in his locker – but when he walked through the shortcut in Unitas Crescent to complete his errand for his colleagues, on the night that Margaret was murdered, he was not wearing overalls.

I had a question for Laura.

I wanted to know more about William, her father who had passed away. William had given George a lift back from work on the Saturday morning, some twelve to fifteen hours after the murder had happened. I asked Laura to tell me everything she could that her father had said to her about the journey he had shared with George on that critical morning. Laura said that her father had described George as acting completely normally and had said nothing at all about the murder in the car ride home to Carluke. In other words, George didn't know anything about the murder until he had returned to the town and nor did Laura's father. There was nothing out of the ordinary. Nothing at all. George had only started to talk about the murder later that day, once he was back in Unitas Crescent. I asked Laura if her father had been interviewed by the police about this interaction and she said that he had, but he was not asked to give evidence at George's trial.

This car journey seems important in establishing what George's behaviour and demeanour were like in the hours immediately after the murder, as the killer would undoubtedly still have been emotionally high. More than this, given that we know George was a teller of tall tales, are we really to believe he would have resisted the temptation to mention that he had seen Margaret, or shared that he had heard noises that had made him frightened, or had seen blood on the route to the station? These details – if they are even true – only emerged later, and then eventually became detailed and graphic over the course of George's various interviews with the police.

I could sense that everyone was getting a bit fidgety and that they wanted me to move on. So I said, 'OK. Let me tell you about my exchange with John Smith.'

I explained all about my abortive first visit, and then the circumstances of my second and successful encounter. I described how Smith looked physically, the lead-up to our conversation on his doorstep and how I had had to dash round the corner after he had closed the door on me to write up my notes, sitting on the wet pavement. There was some laughter at the thought of my trousers getting soaked through.

Having set the scene, I read out my exchange with Smith, including my editorials as to when he had smiled, or when his voice had risen. Everyone listened in total silence, including the couple sitting at the table by the window, although to be fair they did look slightly bemused, and to this day I have no idea if they actually knew anything about what was being discussed. Perhaps they thought we were rehearsing for a play. It was the most attentive audience that I have ever had.

However, as I was reading the interaction, something just didn't seem right. It was as if the act of reading aloud had made me reflect differently on the conversation and that reflection struck a discordant note in my thinking. My audience didn't seem to notice, but it troubled me; it jarred in my consciousness and wouldn't go away. I carried on nonetheless and reached the end:

'And then he closed the door.'

I had finished my soliloquy.

I put down my notebook and looked around the room. At first there was silence.

'So, what do you make of all that?' I asked, unnerved by the unusual quiet.

Still no one spoke. I felt slightly alone, as all of the Bake House Café seemed to be lost in their own thoughts. I wondered if I had disappointed them, because they had been hoping for something more – perhaps a confession?

Then, slowly at first, the calm of silence was broken and the café filled with such frantic discussion that I had to tell everyone to slow down or I wouldn't be able to keep up with what they were saying.

*

We talked for over two hours with such varying discussion that I can't hope to convey everything that was said, but I do want to reflect some of the emotion that was expressed, as well as outline a number of the key themes that emerged. Sometimes there was anger; on other occasions laughter. A few bizarre hares were chased, as when Alison mused that if someone was ever to make a film of the Carluke case – prompted by my description of Falkland and *Outlander* – who would play the various members of the Bake House Café sounding board? She wanted Angelina Jolie to play her, but was firmly put in her place by Margaret: 'You're far too old to be played by Angelina Jolie!'

Laura revealed that in another life she would love to be Beth Loftus.

'Who's that?' asked Margo.

'The woman who is the memory expert.'

'Oh, yes,' said Margo, 'I had forgotten all about her.'

I cannot capture all of our conversation in the same way that I have offered a blow-by-blow account of my exchange with Smith on his doorstep and, for one obvious reason, nor do I want to do so. After all, I do not want to prejudice any future investigation or legal proceedings. So I have to be judicious and therefore will only reveal a number of the themes which shaped our discussion. These themes were: Smith's lack of empathy for Margaret, despite his acknowledgement that she had been a friend; mental health issues, which were an inevitable part of our dialogue given Margo's career as a mental health professional and Margaret's work as a nurse; and mounting anger that the case had not been properly investigated at the time. One final theme related to what the women of the Bake House Café would like to see happen next.

Here is a flavour of some of their comments:

'He says he was a friend,' Laura noted about Smith's interview, but she believed him to have been Margaret's boyfriend. 'Why does he not just say that?'

'Yes! Why can't he just admit to that?' Alison replied.

Margaret thought that even if he was just a friend and not a boyfriend 'that interview had no sympathy – even if he said it was sad. That just doesn't ring true.' Maureen took that theme further and said 'bad and sad – that's all he says. It's not very convincing.'

In short, the sounding board did not feel that Smith's comments were sufficient. 'Just because he's repeating the words,' Maureen concluded, 'doesn't make it sound sincere.'

I pushed Laura and Margo about what they knew of the relationship between Margaret and Smith. They might be wrong. However, they were both adamant that, at the time of the murder, there had been talk that it was more than just a friendship. They were resolute that they had been boyfriend and girlfriend, and that Margaret had ended the relationship before beginning her new relationship with Bob. However, even if she had just been a friend, their reading of what he had said was that Smith had shown no sympathy for her. This was pursued further by Margo and Margaret.

Margo thought out loud: 'You know, it might be that his lack of sympathy is the result of his mental health problems,' and she suggested that our conversation on the doorstep was very reminiscent of interviews that she had had with patients who were mentally ill.

'What do you mean?' I asked.

'It's the outbursts,' Margo replied. 'They say that they know nothing and that they can't help you and then they get really angry. But the very next minute you've changed the subject and they're fine again because you are discussing something else. It's like they are following a script and when you follow that script as well that's fine – they're happy to talk to you. It's when you say something that they don't want to hear you see another side to them.' I thought again about being controlled and then out of control.

Margaret described how electroconvulsive therapy (ECT) often affects people's memory and proceeded to muse whether Smith's weight might have had something to do with medication that he had been taking. 'I think,' she said, 'you could interpret everything on that doorstep through mental health and how people look and behave when they have been ill.'

Alison asked rhetorically, 'If you were asked about

something like the work that you did in the 1970s, would you flare up like that, unless you had something to hide?'

This whole line of reasoning resulted in Laura concluding 'I feel sorry for George and Mrs Beattie. I really do. It's a scandal that this has gone on for so long and there's never been justice.'

Margo admitted that she had 'a lump in her throat'; I also noticed a few tears in her eyes. The sadness in the café was tinged with anger – 'I'm just so annoyed that this wasn't sorted out at the time,' said Alison.

Margaret added, 'It makes me so angry.'

I asked her who she was most angry at and she replied, 'Oh, the police and that William Muncie.'

This general sadness for George, and especially for his mother, allowed me to ask what they now thought about his guilt or innocence. No one had changed their views, and if anything their belief in George's innocence had become stronger. I wanted to know what had led them to this conclusion. I was intrigued as to what new information had impressed them, or if there was something they now realised was significant which they hadn't previously considered. In response to this question an array of factors were offered, including: Bob Beveridge's 'odd suspect' being let go without being charged; the general incompetence of the police investigation; the failure of Muncie to disclose details about the lack of human blood on the knife found at the crime scene; the lack of forensic evidence to link George to Margaret; and their new understanding of false confessions and how anyone put under the sort of pressure that George had been under in the police station might easily admit to something that they didn't do.

Some had even attempted their own criminological autopsies; they had walked the crime scene for themselves. Laura especially had come away with new answers to old questions and revealed 'I went back to Unitas Crescent myself and walked into the shortcut and looked at it for the first time in the way you described to us.' This had allowed her 'to understand why the layout of the streets is so important in understanding why the killer was never seen'. She said that she also now appreciated how her father's journey home with George on the morning after the murder was significant, and wanted to know why that had never been put to the jury. 'My dad should have been giving evidence on behalf of George. It's a scandal that he wasn't asked.'

Indeed, the description of the events following the murder was repeatedly described as being 'a scandal'.

The question I was keen to ask was 'What now?' What did they want to happen as a result of what we had been doing, and what was it that they hoped we could achieve?

Their answers to this last question contained some very specific suggestions, as well as touching on some universal themes related to criminal justice. Laura thought that the 'community have spoken but the criminal justice system has remained silent for too long. We need to stand up to them and we need to hope that someone with power wants to act.' This came back to George's innocence and Maureen thought that, on a practical level, the criminal justice system needed to act because 'there's a murderer still going about, because it is clear to me that George didn't kill Margaret'. Alison said that she felt frustrated about 'who has a voice in this country? Who can stand up to the criminal justice system to get this wrong put right?' There were observations too that if the criminal justice system couldn't get things sorted out, then the Bake House Café should set itself up as an informal justice system! This was a humorous aside, rather than a call to arms for vigilante justice.

Above all, despite Laura's worry that 'no one is listening because it has been fifty years' and Maureen's conclusion that 'they don't want to act because they know what Muncie did was wrong', the Bake House Café simply wanted 'justice for George'. They wanted the case re-opened, George exonerated and the stain of conviction removed from his character. The journey they had been on had been cathartic and had helped them, as Margo aptly put it, 'to make sense of what happened in 1973 and begin to understand what went wrong'.

But, though I wanted the same thing, I was concerned that they were going to be accused of bringing things back to the surface and therefore of just re-opening old wounds. Alison thought that most of the direct participants from 1973 were now dead and that very few people in the town actually knew anything about the case. Given the fact that they lived in Unitas Crescent, I was particularly keen to hear Margo and Laura's view on this.

Margo said, 'I have just been telling the truth about what happened – how can that be bad? Why should the truth hurt?'

Laura stated quite bluntly, 'This is a miscarriage of justice and that needs to be put right. My children – they are in their thirties – it is in their interests and everyone else's children's interests, to put this right. We need to get the case re-opened.'

I started to worry that all of this would take time and we had no guarantee that the Scottish criminal justice system would pay attention to anything that we had discovered. I didn't want the Bake House Café to be disappointed, to feel that they had wasted their time. I put it to them, hopefully, that perhaps it had been cathartic not just from trying to understand Margaret's murder and George's wrongful conviction, but also in meeting up regularly, talking through issues and trying to see how we could take action as a group.

Alison readily agreed: 'I've really enjoyed coming together and talking the case through. It gets me out of the house, for one thing.'

There were nods all around at this.

'So,' I continued, 'what more can we do now – not about murder or miscarriage cases but about Carluke, the sad state of the High Street and getting the town back on its feet?'

This question produced a flurry of thoughts and ideas. Laura said, 'I have always wanted to use the Bake House Café as a community base and perhaps as the starting point for a weekly walk.' By using the natural resources and informal walkways that surround the town, 'we could get a group of us to walk some of the nature paths that ring the town before they begin to disappear'.

With her nursing background, Margaret thought that 'getting people to take exercise is a good idea; we're all too sedentary', and she shot a look at Alison as she said this.

Alison didn't seem to notice.

Maureen and Margo wondered if perhaps that might allow us 'to clean up and create a walk in Colonel's Glen', which has a natural beauty but, as I had observed, is now overgrown and has become little more than a dumping ground. 'It is a bit of a mess,' agreed Margo, but 'we could do something about that too'.

There was a general discussion about how one path that

many people currently use could be connected to this proposed walk through Colonel's Glen. Laura suggested that she had 'tried to get the local council interested in this idea some time ago, but they didn't seem interested. We should try again now, and see what they say.' There were encouraging noises made which suggested to me that they would try again, based on their new-found confidence that together they could take a decision to put their ideas into action.

I do not know what might come of these suggestions, or indeed what the response of the Scottish criminal justice system will be to the publication of this book. Will they embrace what we have discovered and see it as enough to re-open the case? I sincerely hope so. However, whatever the response – either positive or negative – there can be no doubt that the Bake House Café are a group of talented, resourceful and entrepreneurial women who, frankly, could change the world if they wanted to put their minds to it. It seems to me that they have begun to see the future as being in their own hands and, as a result, feel empowered to try to make Carluke a better place in which to live and work, through their own and each other's collective effort.

I can't wait to see the fruits of their labours.

I knew that it was time to take my leave. I would see everyone again soon enough – and we made promises to do so – but I was also a little downbeat. It wasn't just that I was saying goodbye, but also to do with the fact that my reading had left me with a worry.

*

I'd always known that I wanted to end my research in Carluke Library. Libraries are important democratic and cultural centres and even now I am a member of three – the British Library and Cambridge and Birmingham City university libraries. My understanding of their personal and wider significance started when I was a child, sitting in the old Rankin Library. It was there that I borrowed my first books and, perhaps more importantly, it was the very first institution that I was able to join in my own name as an individual – as a unique human being with agency. It was a place where I could assert my identity, as much as it was also about promoting reading and learning.

I remember everything about the Rankin Library. From the paintings on the walls and the smell in the toilets, to the shelves that were reserved for children's books and those which were jealously guarded for adults. This physical description might seem a bit grim, but status within the library marked an evolutionary stage in my life when I was allowed to borrow books that were seen as being for adults only. Even now I remember the solid, square brown ticket that designated me as a member and which was taken and placed in a wooden box filled with other solid, square brown tickets each time I borrowed a book. I learned not to read too quickly, as it was one of the library's rules that a book could not be returned on the same day that it had been borrowed. I recall the titles of many of those borrowed books and the authors who inspired me. At first it was Conan Doyle and then Dickens, before they made way for D. H. Lawrence and Thomas Hardy, although this makes me sound far too serious. I remember only too well going through a phase of reading everything written by a once popular Tory gothic author called Dennis Wheatley – dubbed 'the prince of thriller writers' – who wrote novels about black magic, Satanism and the occult. It was enjoyable pulp fiction.

That space was important to me no matter what I read, and so I return to talk at Carluke Library whenever I am asked as a gesture of my appreciation for the part that it played in my past.

If libraries were to disappear tomorrow, I would regard civilisation as having come to an end.

This statement might be prophetic. Between 2010 and 2019 478 libraries have been closed in England, Wales and Scotland, and in 2018 alone 130 public libraries closed their doors. The Scottish-American industrialist Andrew Carnegie, born in 1835, said that 'a library outranks any other one thing a community can do to benefit its people. It's a never-failing spring in the desert.' I'd agree, but perhaps these library closures might be better seen using a different metaphor – they are a canary in the coalmine. They are closing because local government simply doesn't have the money to keep them open. Their austerity-ridden priorities are focused on providing other services.

I walked away from the Bake House Café and headed back down the High Street towards Rankin Gait. The automatic doors to the 'lifestyle centre' swooshed opened as I walked up to them and I soon found myself in the library.

On entering I was spotted by the senior librarian, Carol Main, who offered me a cup of tea.

Carol went off to put the kettle on and I started to tap out the number on my mobile phone.

Gone are the days of no talking in libraries and so I was free to call the forensic psychologist from my academic sounding board.

My colleague and I have interviewed hundreds of offenders and people who are suspected of having committed crimes. This is often done when we have been asked to consider whether or not these offenders are suitable for parole. Over the years we have become used to the rhythms and patterns of what people say in these circumstances. We have also got used to the typical themes that people will touch upon and, in particular, the games that some offenders will play – their obfuscations, denials and the way that they will want to discuss anything other than the direct question they have been asked. Based on these interviews, both of us have had to form judgements and make some sort of recommendation. That recommendation might lead to the person whom we have been talking to being arrested, or let go without charge; kept in prison, or released on parole to get on with the rest of their lives.

The conclusions we come to are rarely based on a one-off interview, but are usually made after reviews of documents related to the person we are speaking to, about the crime that has been committed, or even after follow-up interviews to clarify certain issues. We might have become good at reading body language and adept at seeing and interpreting non-verbal clues, but there is no magic to what we do and there are no sure-fire 'tells' that will let you know if someone is telling the truth.

That said, lying in an interview is much more taxing on the memory than telling the truth. Telling the truth merely involves retrieving and reconstructing a memory of something that happened, but a lie involves having to invent new stories or, at the very least, develop stories that are available in your memory to accommodate the lies you want to tell. The story that you then tell has to be plausible and can't contradict what has been said previously, or which is already known to the person conducting the interview. That places far greater strain on the memory, and the longer the lie persists, the greater the burden becomes. As a result, an interviewee's responses will become slower, or be spoken with hesitations, pauses, or might even result in speech errors. Listening out for these types of answers is usually a good indication of whether what is being described can be relied upon.

Finally, the interviewer's judgement about what is being said has to be based on the realities of the case and the circumstances in which the crime took place. This judgement is often an art as much as it is a science. That art ironically includes the ability to suspend judgement and establish some form of rapport with the person being interviewed. That wasn't really possible with Smith. To use a crime analogy, my interview with him was much more like a smash-and-grab raid on a jeweller's shop rather than a carefully planned bank robbery. I took what I could, but was that enough to really form a judgement?

The typical themes that will dominate discussions with people who have murdered, are suspected of having murdered someone, or have committed another serious crime, include anger, shame and losing face, and so hitting out to regain a sense of who they were before whatever it was that happened took away their feelings of agency and control. Their target is usually known to them, but does not actually have to have caused the perpetrator harm at all, although that will not be how the attacker will perceive things. Their rage is so great that when they attack they can lose control completely, which is often why overkill occurs. In turn, when they regain control the perpetrator will often block out what has happened because the reality of what they have done is so overwhelming that to acknowledge it would be catastrophic to their sense of self. This is when we say that murderers are 'in denial'. Being 'in denial' is often accompanied by the opposite of losing control: the murderer will become over-controlled and carefully scripted. Occasionally that script will involve the perpetrator blaming someone else and explaining that they either had no role or only a trivial one in the murder.

Murder is a diverse phenomenon and the psychology behind what might have motivated one human being to take the life of another is never simple, or straightforward.

I had already briefed my colleague about the Carluke case and had debated it with him and the other two members of the academic sounding board on a number of occasions. He was therefore expecting me to discuss with him what Smith had said on the doorstep. I wondered if he'd have the same views as me and the same nagging doubt.

I stood in Carluke Library listening to the phone ring, hoping my colleague was in his office and not in the middle of meetings with students. Thankfully, he picked up and was free. I quickly explained all about my abortive first visit and then read out the exchange on the doorstep for a second time. Despite this speaking role, I was keen to listen to what my colleague had to say and noted down his observations in response to each section of dialogue that I read out.

DW: Mr Smith?
JS: That's right.

DW: I've come a long way to talk to you.

JS: No. No. My sister and my brother-in-law wrote to you. I don't want to talk to you. These things are in my past and I'm not well. I can't help you.

FORENSIC PSYCHOLOGIST [FP]: So, this isn't a secret. He's thought this through and so you didn't catch him unawares. You did let people know that you were researching the case and obviously you had written to him. You also left him a note. He's going to speak to you on the basis of how he's thought this through with his family.

DW: I'm sorry, have you not been well?

JS: I'm no [*sic*] going into that; that's my business. I wish you well with your book, but I can't help you at all.

DW: I was writing about Carluke in the 1970s and especially about what happened to Margaret McLaughlin.

JS: Yes, a sad case.

DW: So, that's what I was interested in talking to you about. What are your memories of the murder?

JS: Well I'm no [*sic*] getting involved in that.

DW: OK. I understand. I did get the letter. Thank you—

JS: Beattie murdered Margaret McLaughlin.

That is fact. I can tell you that is fact but I can't go into any details. [His voice rises] Beattie definitely murdered Margaret McLaughlin.

FP: He's overstating things; he comes across as a broken record. Repeating, repeating, repeating. Isn't that like the murder itself? Nineteen stab wounds? He's not going to let you open up areas and be drawn into territory that he doesn't want to discuss. He hasn't rehearsed those areas. This is going to be on his terms. I get the impression that he's confident about his script and that's why he didn't slam the door in your face.

DW: OK. OK. [Trying to calm him down] Well thank you for that. I've been looking for you for quite a wee while. Everyone in Carluke thought that you had emigrated to Canada, so I have even been looking for you there! [I laugh].

JS: No, I didn't go to Canada [He smiles].

DW: I just needed someone to talk about the murder, that was what I wanted to discuss but I understand if you can't speak to me.

JS: I can't get into it but what happened was very very sad and very very bad. She didn't deserve that.

DW: You went out with her for a wee while, didn't you?

JS: No! [Voice rises again] I was a friend of
     hers; I didn't go out with her.

FP: He's creating a distance between himself and the
     murdered girl. Did he date her?

DW: You were just a friend?
JS: She lived around the corner. She had a
     boyfriend. [Pause] He . . .
DW: . . . Bob?
JS: Yes. He went to South Africa and got a
     house there. It was Beattie. I can't tell you
     anything but her brothers Eddie and John
     [his teeth start to chatter] they definitely
     know that Beattie murdered Margaret
     McLaughlin. I can't talk about it. I'm not
     bringing it out. It's up to people in authority
     to bring it out. I'm just low down the scale.
     I'm just an Indian.

FP: This is odd; very odd; I wasn't expecting that.
     Let me come back to that. Go on with the rest of
     what was said.

DW: I spoke with a number of your former
     neighbours from Unitas Crescent. I was
     intrigued by their description of you. 'You
     would have looked twice at him; he was
     very handsome.'

JS: I don't know about that. [He smiles]

DW: That was how Laura and Margo remembered you – as a handsome man. Margo was a runner.

JS: I've got a very bad memory, especially concerning my past. I can't even have a conversation with you about these people. I have no memory. I just have to get on by myself now. Margaret McLaughlin was definitely murdered by Beattie. That is a fact; that is fact. A fact. [Voice rises as he says this]

FP: This seems like blocking things out to me. You and I know that isn't so uncommon. His having no memory is a way to protect himself, as much as it might be to do with the fact that perhaps he's on medication. It is also interesting that he is capable now of living by himself. He's stable – he can get on by himself. That probably wasn't always the case.

DW: OK. I'm grateful that you came to the door.

JS: I can't go into detail about what I was doing, or anything like that. I've just got myself now and [names sister] and I'm taking it nice and easy. It's coming up to fifty years!

DW: Did you work, Mr Smith? After Wishaw High School, what work did you do?

JS: I'm no [sic] going into that [voice rises]. If

you are interested in Margaret McLaughlin
I can say that Beattie definitely murdered
Margaret McLaughlin and her brothers will
confirm that. Beattie writes incessantly –
even now he says that he never murdered
Margaret McLaughlin. He's done his time,
why does he not just say that he did it?

DW: Perhaps because he didn't. There are
people in the town who think that you did.

JS: I don't know what happened. He definitely
did it [voice rises again]. They got the right
man. I wish you well with your book. As
time goes on you will realise why I can't
talk to you.

FP: Oh, yes! I would take that literally – he doesn't
know what happened. For me it suggests that he lost
control. He doesn't know what happened to him!

DW: I think that I know a wee bit about what
happened to you [he says something which
I could not make out]. I know a wee bit
about your time in Hartwood. Are you not
well at the moment?

JS: No, at the moment I am good.

DW: Good?

JS: My sister and my brother-in-law are there
for me. I'm just on my own in that wee
house. I can't help you. [Closes door]

I asked my colleague about what had struck him most about the exchange. He picked up on the two phrases I was most fixated on: 'I don't know what happened'; and when Smith said he was just an 'Indian', and that it was 'up to people in authority to bring it out'. This latter statement was not an answer that we expected to hear in these circumstances.

'That's really odd,' he said, and 'I think that changes the spin on some things.'

I wanted him to be specific and so asked for clarification, especially as I had come to the same conclusion when I had read this statement aloud in the Bake House Café.

'Well,' he continued, 'it implies to me that there is a whole level of understanding about the murder that we just don't have knowledge of. It's such a strange phrase to use that it strikes as being authentic. What is it that people in authority know that he's aware of and it is up to them to reveal?'

I suggested that this might simply have been Muncie – someone 'in authority' – trying to stop gossip in the town when it became clear that people did not believe that George was the culprit; that something was said in private to the McLaughlin family to give them the confidence that George was the guilty man. There was a weakness in this analysis which my colleague immediately pointed out.

'Well, how does Smith know that if it was said to the McLaughlins?'

I had to admit that I didn't know the answer to that question, without myself offering a conspiracy theory. Perhaps we have to accept that is possible?

My colleague added, 'That phrase does change things, doesn't it?'

I think he's right.

I really had wanted things to be neat, despite being acutely aware that they rarely are where murder is concerned. I wanted my conclusions to be obvious and clear cut, but it has not turned out like that. What clouds things is this added layer of mystery that Smith has introduced; a layer that takes me beyond the *dramatis personae* of the murder and into new territory. Has there been a cover-up, over and above what we know happened to George? Did something else happen on the night that Margaret was murdered that involved decisions being taken during the investigation – presumably by Muncie – that serve to confuse the narrative of what had occurred and of the investigation that followed? George Beattie was still to be the fall guy, but Smith's insistence that he was just an 'Indian' and it was for other people in authority to bring things out, was both unexpected and so persistent that it cannot be ignored. In my experience this type of statement does not appear in the scripts of guilty men, or those who are suspected of murder. It is odd and must give me pause for thought.

So, at the end of this journey, what should I conclude?

As far as the investigation into Margaret's murder is concerned, burned police notebooks, inter-force jealousies, lying about forensic evidence and the obvious fitting-up of George might all be better accommodated within a narrative that takes us into the territory of conspiracy and Hollywood, rather than confirmation bias, cock-ups and Lanarkshire. Would it also explain the persistent reluctance of the Scottish criminal justice system to exonerate George, because to re-open the case would be to reveal the depth and extent of that conspiracy to protect the actual culprit? I am not a conspiracy theorist. However, even at the start of this journey I wondered if Muncie had tried to backtrack from his dogged pursuit of George, and later I found it difficult to make sense of the 'bloodstained overalls' email that was sent to me. Who could make that sort of scenario up? Who did these overalls belong to, if they had existed? They certainly weren't George's.

My doorstep conversation with John Smith may have made the Carluke case more difficult to understand, in terms of explaining the investigation.

But what about Smith himself? If I was asked to make a recommendation about his role in the murder, what would I say?

No matter what the gossip in the town might have been, I have never been engaged in a witch hunt and I have been guided throughout by evidence as it emerged over the course of my research. To me, that evidence indicates that, at the very least, Smith has a case to answer and that he should be formally interviewed under caution about Margaret's murder. He has twice failed to deny that he murdered Margaret and his use of the phrase 'I don't know what happened' is so ambiguous that it is imperative that it is pursued further. That can now only be done formally, if and when the case is re-opened.

I sincerely hope it is.

Back in Carluke Library, Carol re-appeared with the tea, and also a plate of biscuits. She put the tea and then the biscuits down on the table, obviously aware that I was deep in thought.

I looked up at her and smiled, and then, pointing at the biscuits, she said, 'It's a bribe! I'm after a favour.'

I grabbed a biscuit and said, 'Ask! What can I do?'

'When the book comes out,' said Carol, smiling broadly, 'will you come back to the library and give us another talk?'

I readily agreed.

At the End of the Road in Carluke

I have my own confession to make.

As I was driving south, away from Scotland and in the cold light of day, it struck me that I was never going to be able to prove 'beyond reasonable doubt' who had murdered Margaret McLaughlin.

'Beyond reasonable doubt' is the standard of proof that would be required to convict a defendant in a court of law. I had to accept that I could not pass that legal test. I do not have access to any relevant forensic evidence related to the murder (if indeed any still exists) and which might be tested using new techniques; or the surviving case files; nor even the notebooks of the investigating officers. Nor, in all fairness, could I be an investigator, the prosecutor, judge and jury all at the same time; that's why every criminal justice system has to have checks and balances: one part of the system independently assessing the work of all the other parts. My search and what I had discovered might have been cathartic for me, my sisters and their friends, but the Bake House Café is not the High Court of Justiciary, Scotland's highest criminal court.

Proof in that context has still to come.

Nevertheless, I hope that I have been able to demon-strate – far beyond reasonable doubt – that George Beattie was not Margaret's killer. Accepting that fact is the first step in discovering who the true culprit was. If Police Scotland was to treat this murder as unsolved, as a cold case that they subjected to a critical review, they would be able to access the various materials which have eluded me in my search. I have absolutely no doubt that in doing so they would be able to identify the real murderer. After all, by myself and with my own limited resources, I have been able to uncover new mate-rials, witnesses whose testimony was never heard and other forms of evidence related to what happened on the night that Margaret was murdered.

Yet to treat this as a 'cold case' the Scottish criminal jus-tice system would have to exonerate George. It would have to admit that it got this wrong. Ironically, I have spent some time considering why there might have been silence and denial in Carluke, but I have not really been able to consider why that denial still permeates Scotland's justice system. They have previous in that respect though, as anyone with knowledge of the case of the former Scottish detective Shirley McKie, and that of the disputed conviction of Abdelbaset Al-Megrahi for his part in the Lockerbie bombing would know. As these two cases reveal, Scottish officialdom can often find it difficult to admit when they've made a mistake.

The Scottish criminal justice system's appeals process seems to have become trapped in a bureaucratic mindset. However, in the Carluke case justice hasn't so much been blind but wilfully blinkered; it appears to be listening but it hasn't really heard. At times, I have been left wondering if it only cares about the *appearance* of justice, rather than with justice's reality. The reality is that they convicted the wrong man. Exonerating George would, at the very least, serve as a very small compensation for all the time that he spent inside. More than this, his exoneration would mark the beginning of a search for the actual culprit and therefore the possibility of justice for Margaret too.

And when the real culprit is convicted, there might even be justice for Carluke.

So there's a lot at stake, but surely every criminal justice system must – has to be – capable of meeting these challenges?

I really do hope that the Scottish criminal justice system is both capable and willing to meet these tests, for we all need a criminal justice system that we can respect, although I would find it difficult to respect a system that stubbornly refuses to acknowledge George's innocence. I worry that the failure to correct this egregious wrong reveals that the criminal justice system only works for those with power and not for those who are powerless, or who come from what is sometimes seen as the 'wrong side' of town. Justice needs to work for Unitas Crescent, as much as it might for the more salubrious West Avenue.

My journey has been a search for the truth – specifically a search for the truth about a killer's identity – and I am ready and willing to share all of my research with any future investigation. However, this journey has been, from the very start, about something much broader. This was also a search to discover a mechanism that would allow a community to find its voice and express itself in defence of the common good. I see in collective action hope and optimism; a belief that anything is possible when we act together and in solidarity. It is the opposite of apathy, pessimism and hopelessness, and a retort to those who think that both individual and collective human agency don't matter.

They do.

They matter deeply. There really is something called 'society' and when people pool their knowledge, resources and skills and act in concert, they can actively shape what that society looks like.

At the end of the road in the Carluke case, the message I take away is that to exist – what it means to be human; what it means to be 'us' – is to be engaged, informed and involved. I cannot regenerate Carluke's High Street and fill it once more with thriving shops, instead of charity shops and a food bank, and I doubt that it is ever going to be the setting for a popular American TV drama that will bring tourists in its wake. What I *can* do is engage in a public debate that questions who benefits from an economic system that prioritises global corporate profits at the cost of individual or community misery. I can criticise why we tacitly accept that our GDP should increase year on year, without ever questioning the few who benefit from that annual increase – and those who do not. Our current economic arrangements are a form of systemic violence, as opposed to the subjective, interpersonal violence which is the reality of murder. We need to recognise that this systemic violence not only does harm, but is also the driving and in-built feature of our economic system which serves to widen the gap between rich and poor, the weak and the powerful. That system is neither neutral nor natural, but is clearly ideological and so to do something about it we can speak and write; discuss, debate and lecture; mobilise, march and protest; I can vote; and, above all, we can give a damn.

Is that enough? Perhaps we are fast reaching the stage when it's not, and so at the end of this road I feel a sense of failure.

Above all else, I am sorry I have not yet been able to get justice for Margaret, or for her family. And what of Margaret herself? Her life was brutally cut short. She never got to pursue a career, or to marry Bob, settle down and have children and then watch those children grow, get married and then have children themselves. She deserved so much more than what her short life delivered to her. It is in her memory that this book has been written and while I'm certain that she would have wanted the legacy that comes from a life lived fully, I hope there is a small crumb of consolation in that she remains in our thoughts.

Margaret has been the catalyst for a community to come together and, in doing so, to make public what some of us knew privately in 1973. If the Scottish Police had done their job at the time, this book would never have needed to be written. By being that catalyst, in allowing Carluke to find its voice, Margaret's legacy is therefore one that also transcends the personal and becomes political. She is at the centre of an ongoing civic drama that seeks to regain a sense of what is right and what is wrong, and how institutions need to be held publicly accountable and admit when they make mistakes. Hers is a legacy that encourages, enables and favours people at the grass roots of our society – in the Bake House Café, Unitas Crescent, Carluke Library and in the High Street – rather than those who have money and power; a legacy that champions engagement and democracy over complacency and authoritarianism in public life. The legacy of Margaret's tragedy is the moral heart of an insistence to become who it is that we would like to be as individuals, and of an understanding about how to act collectively so that we can be a better community than we have been in the past.

Every drama needs an appropriate ending, and I hope that we are all now much closer to a fitting, formal and legal resolution as to what really did happen on the night of Friday 6 July 1973.

This book has always been a journey into the past and of using what we found there to right some shocking and wicked injustices. In doing so it has also been about a community thinking about itself, its values and its place in the world; about marking out what it wants to be and now to be known for. That's a form of civic re-generation too.

Of course we link the past to the present in a variety of ways, both publicly and in private. Chief among the former are monuments and memorials. All too often these are about the men of our communities who have come to be viewed as the 'great and the good'.

Perhaps the town's Market Place is already too full of monuments and memorials to the men who are seen as being our best and brightest. That's for other people to decide. However, wouldn't it be fitting to remember more formally – and in public – a quiet, ordinary and reserved young woman who lost her life? More than fitting, wouldn't it be right to remember this woman and her part in the town's history? After all, we choose to honour those from our past whom we think will inspire future generations and whose lives celebrate the values that we hold most dear, so why not honour Margaret?

I'd like to think that Dr Rankin would agree.

A Short Guide to Further Reading and
A Note on Sources

As far as I am aware, this is the first book about the murder of Margaret McLaughlin, although I have drawn attention in the text to a number of newspaper articles about the case. Nor has the miscarriage of justice that saw George Beattie wrongly convicted of her murder been the subject of a book. However, the case was featured in a BBC *Rough Justice* documentary and, as a good starting point for someone coming fresh to the case, there is an excellent website, www.roughjusticetv.co.uk, which offers a comprehensive analysis of the police investigation, George's pseudo-confession, his trial, conviction and subsequent appeals. These various appeals and the reason for their rejection can be found on the Scottish Courts and Tribunals website, www.scotcourts.gov.uk. They were also widely covered in a number of Scottish newspapers.

I do not pretend to be an expert in Scottish history and so I accept that I might be mistaken, or perhaps simply over-stating the case. However, I was disappointed by how little was written about lowland Scotland's history, especially in

comparison to the 'big three' of Scottish historiography –
Glasgow, Edinburgh and, especially, the Highlands. I therefore
relied on the two volumes produced by T. C. Smout, *A History
of the Scottish People* (London: Fontana Press, 1972) – which
has been reprinted on many occasions – and the much more
recent account by T. M. Devine, *The Scottish Clearances: A
History of the Dispossessed* (London: Allen Lane, 2018), which
discusses lowland Scotland throughout. The various bodies
that make up the Scottish criminal justice system are usefully
outlined on the website www.gov.scot and a good academic
introductory textbook is H. Croall, G. Mooney, M. Munro
(eds), *Criminal Justice in Scotland* (Cullompton: Willan, 2013).
For ease of reference, criminal justice is about a society's
formal response to crime and then is 'defined more specifically in terms of a series of decisions and actions taken by a
number of agencies in response to a specific crime or criminal
or crime in general. Following the recognition of a crime-like
incident, or in seeking to prevent lawless behaviour, criminal
justice agencies become involved' – M. Davies, H. Croall and
J. Tyrer, *Criminal Justice* (London: Longman, 1998). These
agencies would include, at least, law enforcement such as the
police, the courts and the penal system.

A useful starting point for anyone interested more academ-
ically in murder remains Fiona Brookman's *Understanding
Homicide* (London: Sage, 2005), which can be augmented by
Shani D'Cruze, Sandra Walklate and Samantha Pegg's *Murder*
(Cullompton: Willan, 2006). More recently Elizabeth Yardley,
whom I mention in the text, has produced a more contempo-
rary take on the subject in her *Social Media and Homicide
Confessions: Stories of Killers and their Victims* (Bristol: Policy

Press, 2017). I wrote about my work with a number of murderers in *My Life With Murderers* (London: Sphere, 2019), and in this professional biography I describe murder as a slippery phenomenon and murderers and their accompanying psychology as diverse and different from one another as trees in a forest. I also discuss the importance of the doorstep to contact killers. My suspicions about people who have no 'digital footprint' were formed through reading Nancy K. Baym, *Personal Connections in the Digital Age* (Cambridge: Polity Press, 2015).

For forensic psychology, a few helpful starting points are Ray Bull et al., *Criminal Psychology* (Oxford: Oneworld, 2009); Adrian J. Scott, *Forensic Psychology* (London: Palgrave, 2010); and Peter Ainsworth, *Psychology and Crime: Myths and Reality* (Harlow: Longman, 2000). David Canter's *Forensic Psychology: A Very Short Introduction* (Oxford: Oxford University Press, 2010) is also worth consulting, given that Canter is the guiding light within investigative psychology. An early secondary work that explains the original approach to crime scene analysis is R. Holmes and S. Holmes, *Profiling Violent Crimes: An Investigative Tool* (Sage: Thousand Oaks, 1996), and remains of interest as it reveals how investigative psychology differs. I mention Nicholas Groth, *Men who Rape: The Psychology of the Offender* (New York: Plenum Press, 1979), which he wrote with Jean Birnbaum, in the text. There are a number of good introductions to criminology, including A. Liebling, S. Maruna and L. McAra (eds), *The Oxford Handbook of Criminology*, which is currently in its sixth edition, and James Treadwell, *Criminology: The Essentials* (London: Sage, 2006). Treadwell, one of my former PhD students and now Professor of Criminology at the University of

Staffordshire, is an 'ultra realist' and therefore comes from a very different academic tradition than Liebling *et al.*

Beth Loftus's work on false memories is best outlined in *The Myth of Repressed Memory: False Memories and Allegations of Sexual Abuse* (New York: St Martin's Press, 1995), which she wrote with Katherine Ketcham, and, in this country, false confessions have been written about most scientifically by Aldert Vrij of the University of Portsmouth in *Detecting Lies and Deceit: The Psychology of Lying and its Implications for Professional Practice* (Oxford: Wiley-Blackwell, 2000). I also used the notes that I took from Loftus's lecture, 'The Fiction of Memory', which she delivered in London in January 2019. I have also mentioned Jim Trainum's *How the Police Generate False Confessions: An Inside Look at the Interrogation Room* (Lanham, Maryland: Rowman & Littlefield, 2016). Both Trainum and Loftus feature in a series of short American films about *The Psychological Phenomena That Can Lead to Wrongful Convictions*, which can be found at www.inno-cenceproject.org. I mention the cases of Steven Avery and Brendan Dassey, which featured in the Netflix series *Making a Murderer*. The best account of these cases is found in Jerome Buting, *Illusion of Justice: Inside Making a Murderer and America's Broken System* (New York: HarperCollins, 2017).

There is a lively academic debate about the existence of 'police culture' – or perhaps police 'cultures' – and what this/these might look like. A good way into this territory is through Robert Reiner, *The Politics of the Police* (Hemel Hempstead: Harvester Wheatsheaf, 1992), and comparing what Reiner posits with P. A. J. Waddington in *Policing Citizens* (London: UCL Press, 1999). I review all of this in D. Wilson, J. Ashton and D. Sharp, *What Everyone in Britain Should Know About the Police* (Oxford: Oxford University Press, 2001). We conclude that the police do have elements of a distinctive police culture (and we accept that there are distinct working cultures within other criminal justice organisations too) and which would include: a tendency towards action; cynicism; conservatism; suspicion; prejudice; pragmatism; and, finally, a sense of mission.

I used William Muncie, *The Crime Pond: Memoirs of William Muncie formerly Assistant Chief Constable of Strathclyde Police* (Glasgow: Chambers, 1979) throughout the text, and also contrasted Muncie with John Du Rose and his *Murder Was My Business: The Whole Truth by Britain's Most Feared Detective* (St Albans: Mayflower, 1971). The case of Peter Manuel is described in A. M. Nicol, *Manuel: Scotland's First Serial Killer* (Edinburgh: Black & White Publishing, 2008). Manuel's crimes and Muncie's investigation were dramatised in a TV series called *In Plain Sight*, which was broadcast on ITV in 2016. The extraordinary meeting between Manuel and William Watt is the basis of Denise Mina's 2017 true crime novel *The Long Drop* (London: Vintage) in which she describes the Lanarkshire Police as 'a Masonic Lodge with truncheons'. She also describes Muncie as 'a beefy, square-jawed man. He has a military bearing and speaks like an angry sergeant major. He hates chaos and disorder and things not going the way he wants.' The part of William Muncie in *In Plain Sight* was played by the Scottish actor Douglas Henshall and it is worth considering if this excellent actor remotely resembles the man that both Mina and I describe. In passing, I alluded to a serial killer dubbed 'Jack the Stripper' by the press, and a good introduction to that case is Robin Jarossi, *The Hunt for the 60s' Ripper* (London: Mirror Books, 2017). In his memoir John Du Rose tried to claim that he knew the identity of Jack the Stripper all along. He did not – but this serves to illustrate just how much his failure to catch this killer had damaged his reputation.

I describe a number of social psychology experiments throughout the book. Social psychology is typically defined as 'the attempt to understand and explain how the thoughts, feelings and behaviour of individuals are influenced by the actual, imagined or implied presence of other human beings' – G. Allport, 'The Historical Background of Modern Social Psychology' (1954). The experiments that I harness in the text are related to Milgram's 'obedience to authority' research, the 'bystander calculus' and the 'smoke-filled room' experiment. Tom Butler-Bowden's *50 Psychology Classics* (London: John Murray Press, 2017) is a quick way to get an overview of some the relevant materials, as is Paul Seager, *Social Psychology: A Complete Introduction* (London: Hodder & Stoughton, 2014). The 'smoke-filled room' experiment was first outlined by B. Latane and J. Darley in 'Group Inhibition of Bystander Intervention in Emergencies', *Journal of Personality and Social Psychology*, 10:3 (1968), 215–21, and which involved a group of male undergraduates, after Latane and Darley became interested in the subject as a result of the 1964 murder of Kitty Genovese. This case has been the subject of a number of studies, but most recently Catherine Pelonero, *Kitty Genovese: A True Account of a Public Murder and Its Private Consequences* (New York: Skyhorse Publishing, 2014). The 'bystander calculus' experiments/model were first outlined in I. M. Piliavin, J.

Rodin and J. Piliavin, 'Good Samaritanism: An Underground Phenomenon?', *Journal of Personality and Social Psychology*, 13:2 (1969), 289–99. Finally, there is the monumental work of Stanley Milgram, *Obedience to Authority: An Experimental View* (New York: Harper & Row, 1974).

In describing my criminological autopsy I used the term 'psychogeography'. This is now more commonly called 'deep topography' and the protagonists of both share roots with the *flâneur* of nineteenth-century Paris – a figure much loved (and frankly overused) by academics and cultural commentators. Of course the *flâneur* wandered aimlessly about the streets, silently observing all before him, whereas within my criminological autopsy I have a very specific aim and purpose. A good introduction to this subject matter is Merlin Coverley, *Psychogeography* (Harpenden: Oldcastle Books, 2018) and, as a practitioner and populariser, Will Self's *Psychogeography* (London: Bloomsbury, 2007) is also useful.

I refer to Hartwood Hospital on a number of occasions and to SUMP, the Scottish Union of Mental Patients. I used Mark Gallagher's 2017 doctoral thesis from the University of Glasgow to build an understanding of this movement, but all of this can be more easily followed in a subsequent article which he produced, called 'From Asylum to Action in Scotland: The Emergence of the Scottish Union of Mental Patients, 1971–1972', *History of Psychiatry*, 28:1 (2017), 101–14. I mention schizophrenia a number of times and consulted various websites to get a better understanding of this mental illness, especially www.nhs.uk. My comments about the link between schizophrenia and violence were shaped in particular by reading Elizabeth Walsh, Alec Buchanan and Thomas

Fahy, 'Violence and Schizophrenia: Examining the Evidence', *British Journal of Psychiatry*, 180:6 (2002), 490–5. A more general overview is provided by R. Shug and H. Fradella, *Mental Illness and Crime* (London: Sage, 2014).

The forensic psychiatrist John MacDonald first suggested, as a result of his clinical observation of one hundred patients, that there was a 'triad' of behaviours – fire-setting, bedwetting and cruelty to animals – that was predictive of future violent behaviour in 'The Threat to Kill', *American Journal of Psychiatry*, 120:2 (1963), 125–30. However, there has been mixed support for this observation. Even so, the FBI came to endorse some of this work. See, for example, R. Ressler, A. Burgess and J. Douglas, *Sexual Homicide Patterns and Motives* (New York: Simon and Schuster, 1988). More recent research can be found in P. Kavanagh, T. Signal and N. Taylor, 'The Dark Triad and Animal Cruelty: Dark Personalities, Dark Attitudes and Dark Behaviours', *Personality and Individual Differences*, 55:6 (2013), 666–70.

There are a number of books about the English theologian William of Ockham, one of the three most important philosophers of the Middle Ages, along with Thomas Aquinas and John Duns Scotus. In a crowded field, I particularly value Rondo Keele, *Ockham Explained: From Razor to Rebellion* (Chicago: Open Court Publishing, 2010), which charts Ockham's rather controversial life, as well as outlining his philosophical approach.

A number of academic works have informed my narrative. These included: Michael Sandel, *What Money Can't Buy: The Moral Limits of Markets* (London: Penguin, 2013); Jock Young, *The Exclusive Society* (London: Sage, 1999);

Slavoj Žižek, *Violence* (London: Profile Books, 2007); and Stan Cohen, *States of Denial: Knowing about Atrocities and Suffering* (Cambridge: Polity Press, 2000). The idea of 'disavowal' in the human psyche was first proposed by Sigmund Freud. Two introductory books about Freudian theory which I have found useful are Stephen Frosh, *A Brief Introduction to Psychoanalytic Theory* (London: Palgrave, 2012) and Michael Kahn, *Basic Freud: Psychoanalytic Thought for the Twenty First Century* (New York: Basic Books, 2002). Please note that Žižek uses disavowal in a different way from Freud, although he too is interested in psychoanalysis – specifically the work of Jacques Lacan. For Žižek, disavowal is 'I know but I don't want to know that I know so I don't know', and he suggests that our whole way of life is based on such ethical compromises. Finally, John Ashton, *Scotland's Shame: Why Lockerbie Still Matters* (Edinburgh: Birlinn, 2013) allowed me to begin to understand the various ways of interpreting what happened in the wake of the Lockerbie bombing.

While not referenced within the text, my main inspiration in thinking about the inherent violence engrained in our economic system comes from reading the work of Professor Steve Hall, the 'godfather' of ultra-realism in criminology. In particular Hall's *Theorising Crime and Deviance: A New Perspective* (London: Sage, 2012) shaped much of my thinking about this, especially something which Hall has described as the historic 'pseudo pacification process', which he explains accompanied capitalism's growth. This work is challenging but a worthwhile and always stimulating read. Of note, Hall has often written with Professor Simon Winlow, whom I mention in the text in relation to his work with violent men.

A good starting point to understand this latter research is Winlow's *Bad Fellas: Crime, Tradition and New Masculinities* (Oxford: Berg, 2001), which as far as I am aware was the first sustained analysis of organised crime and violence, and which uses covert research methods. For a personal account of how the systemic violence of the underlying economic system can structure the pattern of your life in a deprived community, see Darren McGarvey, *Poverty Safari: Understanding the Anger of Britain's Underclass* (London: Picador, 2018). McGarvey's account of growing up in Pollock on the south side of Glasgow won the 2018 Orwell Prize and takes the reader on a journey into a damaged and deprived community.

Most of the archival searches I undertook can be completed online. Particularly useful is www.scotlandspeople.gov.uk and this excellent resource has to be the starting point for anyone interested in research related to Scottish issues. I consulted old-fashioned paper archives in the British Library, which is the only place, in England at least, to have a full run of the *Daily Record*, and where I was able to consult Daniel Rankin Stuert, *Bygone Days: Some Recollections by Daniel Rankin Stuert and Other Family Stories* (Edinburgh: Dunedin Press, 1936). This privately circulated work contained the photograph of Dr Daniel Reid Rankin that I describe in the text. I also used paper archives at Cambridge University Library, who very kindly facilitated finding me a copy of Rankin's *Notices Historical, Statistical & Biographical Relating to the Parish of Carluke from 1288 till 1874* (Glasgow: William Rankin, 1874). Ron Harris at the *Carluke Gazette* arranged for various copies of the relevant editions of the newspaper to be sent to me via Paul Archibald at Lanark Library, which holds a complete run of the newspaper. I was delighted to have been able to use materials held about my home town in Carluke Library.

My major interview sources were my sisters and their three friends. I also briefly interviewed 'John Smith'. I have taken the decision to use a pseudonym and not to describe the specific location where this interview took place, and I have also deliberately obscured some of the details of my visit. My archival research allowed me to build up a detailed picture of Smith, but I have not published all of this material. However, as I have stated within the text, I am happy to make this available if the case should be re-opened. I sometimes interviewed my sisters individually and also informally, but my favourite way to gather information was through my Bake House Café sounding boards, which would often be followed up by a flurry of emails to clarify certain points. I also formally interviewed ten other people, including Bob Beveridge, George Beattie's original solicitor and a number of detectives who had worked on the case, but who would prefer to remain anonymous. Some of these interviews lasted for only fifteen minutes, while others went on for several hours. I also discussed the case regularly with an academic sounding board, which included a forensic psychologist and two criminologists. As one of the three people within this sounding board asked to remain anonymous, I have taken the decision not to name any of them. I also received scores of emails, a handful of letters and took a variety of phone calls from other residents of Carluke who wanted to discuss Margaret's murder. Even after the first draft of the book had been delivered, I was still receiving emails from people who had just heard about my research and wanted to share their stories. One of these correspondents offered me a wonderful insight into Smith, although I have chosen not to include this within the text.

I describe my use of these sources as contributing to my criminological autopsy, and I have also drawn attention to how this has connections to 'ethnography'. A basic introduction to this type of research is John Brewer, *Ethnography* (Buckingham: Open University Press, 2000), while the more adventurous may want to consult Paul Willis, *The Ethnographic Imagination* (Cambridge: Polity Press, 2000). I have discussed this particular research method in a number of peer-review articles and, most recently, in *My Life With Murderers*. The ethical dimension of any work to be undertaken in the field can be found at www.britsoccrim.org and I also found useful Sharon Hayes, *Criminal Justice Ethics: Cultivating the Moral Imagination* (Abingdon: Routledge, 2015)

As I indicate in the text, I chose not to interview members of Margaret McLaughlin's family, George Beattie, or members of his family. I hope that my research brings them a small measure of comfort and that I am forgiven for intruding into their lives.

Acknowledgements

I would like to thank everyone at Curtis Brown and Little, Brown who do so much to support me. As far as the former are concerned I need to mention Jacquie Drewe, Emma Power, Madeleine Newman-Suttle, Luke Speed and, of course, my wonderful literary agent Gordon Wise. At Little, Brown, Kirsteen Astor has always skilfully guided me through the strange world of book festivals and, during the research for this book, even accompanied me for a drink with Beth Loftus. Above all, my stalwart editor Rhiannon Smith has championed the book from the start and shown tenacity and insight, finding exactly the right words of encouragement to keep me going when I thought that I would fail. I also thank Meryl Evans, who had the unenviable task of completing the legal read, and Zoe Gullen. I would like to thank colleagues at Birmingham City University, especially Professors Michael Brookes and Elizabeth Yardley, and also Liam Brolan, Lukas Danos, Laura Riley and Dan Rusu with whom I continue to teach undergraduates about criminological theory on a Thursday. My academic sounding board would prefer to remain anonymous, but I want to acknowledge their help nonetheless. I would also like to thank Professor Elizabeth Loftus – it is always a pleasure to see you – and Simon Winlow and Emma Kelly.

My other sounding board was of course the Bake House Café. I hope that the book that I have produced is all that they would have wanted it to be and I would like to put on record my thanks to Maureen Dickson, Laura McConnell and Margo Morrow. I found all the time that I spent with these women enriching and inspiring, and I hope that I didn't ask them too many questions! My special thanks must go to Laura, who would often open the café just for me, and very patiently told and re-told several aspects of her story. Thanks also to the people of Carluke more generally, especially my brother-in-law William Scoular, various nieces and nephews, my wonderful wife Anne Maguire, who accompanied me on several trips to Carluke, Carol Main at Carluke Library – especially for the biscuits – and for the support that I received from staff at the *Carluke Gazette* and also at Lanark Library. Thanks too to the staff at the British Library, where much of the early research for the book was conducted.

My greatest debt is mentioned in the dedication at the start of this book. It is offered as a small gesture of heartfelt thanks to my sisters for all of their love and support. I know that I am only the man that I have become because of the women that you are. I love you and I know that our parents would be so very proud of all that you have each achieved. You are remarkable people; the best of Scotland.

The Narrative of the Murder of Margaret McLaughlin, and the Police Investigation into her Death. The Disputed Interviews and Charging of George Beattie

Date	Margaret McLaughlin	George Beattie	Police investigation	Rough Justice alternative
Friday 6 July 1973	Leaves home to catch train to Glasgow; at some point during the evening is reported missing when she fails to arrive at her future sister-in-law's house.	Leaves home to buy tomatoes for his work colleagues; seen by a variety of witnesses; goes to work at Lanarkshire Steelworks.		
Saturday 7 July 1973	Margaret's body discovered in Colonel's Glen, although timing is disputed. Various personal items recovered.	GB provides first statement – taken by DS Adam and DC Waddell during their house-to-house enquiries on the morning after GB returned from work. He does not mention seeing Margaret. He makes no mention of the murder on the car journey back to Carluke.	DCS Muncie takes charge of investigation. Knife discovered and removed for forensic testing in presence of pathologist Walter Weir and chief medical officer William McLay.	Margaret's body officially recorded as discovered by Inspector Harry Robson at 1425, but actually found by PC John Baker at 1030.
Sunday 8 July 1973	More items belonging to Margaret recovered after police clear area – for example, her pinkie ring.		Police clear area where Margaret's body had been discovered, and Muncie flies in the *Daily Record* aeroplane.	

Date	Margaret McLaughlin	George Beattie	Police investigation	Rough Justice alternative
Monday 9 July 1973			Aerial photographs of the crime scene published in the *Daily Record*.	
Tuesday 10 July 1973		Second statement of GB taken by DS Adam and DC Waddell, and later that day he recreates his journey to Gorry's in presence of DS Adam and DC Waddell.	GB walks the route with DS Adam and DC Waddell.	The beginning of GB's 'special knowledge' – his awareness of the particular circumstances of Margaret's murder.
Wednesday 11 July 1973	Margaret's fiancé Bob Alexander flies in from South Africa, and he later walks with her brothers – John and Eddie – the route she took on 6 July. This walk is photographed by the *Daily Record*.	GB attends Carluke Police Station and goes over his statement. Later would make a third and then a fourth statement, and would eventually admit to seeing six men stabbing Margaret. Has a mild epileptic fit; is extremely distressed.	DC Semple and PC Mair go over GB's statement. DC Semple begins a sketch of the area where Margaret's body had been discovered. Semple and Mair go off duty, and GB's interview continued by DS Mortimer and DC Johnston; both keep records in their notebooks of the interviews.	DC Semple and PC Mair are seemingly unaware that GB had been taken to the scene of the crime the previous evening. DC Johnston's notebook of the interview was destroyed after he was interviewed by the journalist Peter Hill.

Date	Margaret McLaughlin	George Beattie	Police investigation	Rough Justice alternative
Wednesday 11 July 1973 – *cont.*			DS Mortimer continues with sketch and produces items for GB to view that had belonged to Margaret. DS Mortimer states that GB admitted seeing six men stab Margaret. GB has mild epileptic fit. Ian Hamilton – Scientific Officer – writes to Muncie and states 'no human blood present' in either knife or soil sample.	According to Hill, DC Johnston stated that he did not see any items being brought into the interview room. Hill alleges that DCI Willie Gold continues to interview GB after Mortimer has finished his interview; Gold knew location of Margaret's body, knife and suitcase. The sketch is further developed. GB alleges that Gold made up the story for him of the six men stabbing Margaret. Hamilton's letter about the knife not having 'human blood' on it is not made available to the wider investigation.

Date	Margaret McLaughlin	George Beattie	Police investigation	Rough Justice alternative
Thursday 12 July 1973	Photograph of Bob Alexander appears on page 11 of the *Daily Record* under the headline 'Heartbreak Walk for Murdered Girl's Fiancé'.	GB charged with murder at around 0130, and taken to Lanark Police Station. He mentions the knife, and offers to help the police identify where it had been.	GB returns to Colonel's Glen later that morning, and is alleged to have made incriminating remarks about the knife, and where it was found, to Muncie and Gold. GB charged with murder and taken back to Colonel's Glen, handcuffed to DC Johnston. Makes incriminating remarks about the knife to Muncie and Gold. Another suspect is located in Carluke Police Station, being informally questioned by DC Beveridge and DC Muir of the Scottish Crime Squad. He is released without charge.	DC Johnston does not record any incriminating conversation between GB and Muncie and Gold.
Friday 13 July 1973		GB appears in Lanark Sheriff Court charged with murder. He pleads Not Guilty.